Prophetic Leadership

Transform Your Business with
Sunnah Principles for Lasting Success

SARAH GULFRAZ

Copyright © 2025 Sarah Gulfraz

Sarah Gulfraz has asserted her right to be identified as the author of this Work in accordance with the Copyright, Designs and Patents Act 1988.

All rights reserved.

No portion of this book may be reproduced in any form, stored in a retrieval system, stored in a database, or published/transmitted in any form or by any means, electronic, mechanical, photocopying, recording or otherwise, without prior written permission of the publisher.

Dedication

~ Bismillah ~

May Allah (swt) accept our efforts and grant us success in this life and the next. Ameen.

In dedication to my loving family and all their support.

Contents

1. Introduction to Sunnah Leadership in Business ... 1
2. Integrity and Trustworthiness ... 15
3. Empathy and Compassion ... 44
4. Visionary Leadership and Strategic Planning ... 78
5. Effective Communication Skills ... 97
6. Decision-Making and Problem-Solving ... 118
7. Leading by Example ... 143
8. Building and Nurturing Relationships ... 172
9. Adaptability and Innovation ... 198
10. Legacy and Impact ... 220

Find Out More ... 236

Chapter One

Introduction to Sunnah Leadership in Business

Leading a business today feels like stepping into a dance with the unknown, where the rhythm is dictated by ethics, inclusivity, and the quest for sustainable growth. Balancing these intricate steps can often seem like walking a tightrope in a storm. Yet, amid the chaos, the timeless wisdom of Prophet Muhammad (peace be upon him) offers a guiding star, a beacon that illuminates the path with its profound simplicity and enduring relevance.

Imagine a leader whose influence stems not from authority, but from a deep well of empathy, humility, and unwavering moral principles. This is the essence of Prophet Muhammad's (PBUH) leadership—a style that transcends time and resonates powerfully in today's complex business landscape. His approach was akin to a gentle breeze that carries the scent of blooming flowers, subtle yet profoundly transformative.

Picture this: a company where values like honesty, compassion, and justice are not just words etched on a plaque but are lived experiences, breathed in and out with every decision made. This is the kind of environment that Sunnah-inspired leadership fosters. It is a place where trust is cultivated, not commanded, where customer loyalty blossoms naturally, and where employees feel genuinely valued and inspired to bring their best selves to work every day.

For Muslim entrepreneurs, the teachings of Sunnah offer more than a blueprint for personal growth. They provide a map for creating ripples of positive change that extend far beyond the walls of their businesses, touching communities and reshaping entire industries. In a world driven by profit margins and bottom lines, the prophetic approach offers a delicate balance—a dance between financial success and ethical integrity. This harmony aligns with Islamic teachings, addressing contemporary leadership challenges with a focus on justice, fairness, and social welfare.

By bridging Islamic teachings with contemporary leadership challenges, we reveal the enduring relevance of these principles. As businesses navigate complex global issues, the prophetic model shines as a guiding light, showing that true leadership is about serving others, making ethical choices, and striving for excellence.

Understanding the Prophetic Model of Leadership

Overview of Prophet Muhammad's (PBUH) leadership style

Prophet Muhammad's (PBUH) leadership style remains an inspiring model for contemporary leaders. His approach was a unique blend of wisdom, compassion, and foresight, transcending time and cultural boundaries. The essence of his leadership can be understood through the key principles that defined his actions and decisions.

One of the most defining traits of Prophet Muhammad's (PBUH) leadership was his deep compassion and empathy for others. He led with genuine concern for the well-being of his followers, always considering their needs and feelings. This created a sense of trust and loyalty among his companions. He listened attentively, understood their concerns, and responded with kindness and understanding.

> *"And by the Mercy of Allah, you dealt with them gently. And had you been severe and harsh-hearted, they would have broken away from about you." (Quran 3:159)*

Justice and fairness were also cornerstones of his leadership. He treated everyone equally, regardless of social status, race, or background. His decisions were always based on justice, ensuring that the rights of all individuals were respected. This commitment to fairness strengthened the social fabric and promoted harmony within the community.

> *"O you who have believed, be persistently standing firm in justice, witnesses for Allah, even if it be against yourselves or parents and relatives." (Quran 4:135)*

Integrity and honesty were hallmarks of his character. Known as Al-Amin (the Trustworthy), he consistently demonstrated honesty in his dealings, setting a standard for ethical conduct that leaders today can aspire to.

> *"Give full measure and weight in justice and do not deprive people of their due and do not commit abuse on the earth, spreading corruption." (Quran 11:85)*

Despite his significant influence, the Prophet (PBUH) remained humble and modest. He never sought to elevate himself above others and always recognised the contributions of his companions. His humility made him approachable and relatable, endearing him to those he led.

> *"The servants of the Most Merciful are those who walk upon the earth easily, and when the ignorant address them harshly, they say words of peace." (Quran 25:63)*

He possessed extraordinary vision and foresight, with a clear sense of purpose and direction that he effectively communicated to his followers. His ability to see beyond immediate challenges and focus on long-term goals was instrumental in the successful establishment and expansion of the Muslim community.

> *"Say, 'This is my way; I invite to Allah with insight, I and those who follow me. And exalted is Allah; and I am not of those who associate others with Him.'" (Quran 12:108)*

Leadership often involves navigating through challenges and setbacks. Prophet Muhammad (PBUH) demonstrated remarkable patience and perseverance in the face of adversity, whether dealing with opposition, personal loss, or the trials of leading a nascent community.

> *"So be patient. Indeed, the promise of Allah is truth." (Quran 30:60)*

He understood the importance of delegation and empowerment, entrusting responsibilities to his companions and recognising their strengths and capabilities. This not only alleviated his burden but also developed the skills and confidence of those he led.

> *"And those who have responded to their lord and established prayer and whose affair is [determined by] consultation among themselves..." (Quran 42:38)*

Effective communication was another hallmark of his leadership. He conveyed his messages clearly and succinctly, ensuring his followers understood his instructions and the underlying principles. This helped maintain unity and coherence within the community.

> *"And We did not send any messenger except [speaking] in the language of his people to state clearly for them..."*
> *(Quran 14:4)*

An example of his compassionate leadership is his interaction with a Bedouin who urinated in the mosque. Instead of reacting with anger, the Prophet (PBUH) calmly instructed his companions to clean the area and gently advised the Bedouin about proper conduct. This incident illustrates his patience, empathy, and ability to handle difficult situations with grace and wisdom.

Prophet Muhammad (PBUH) valued the input and contributions of all community members, fostering a culture of consultation and mutual respect. He actively sought the opinions of others, ensuring that all voices were heard and considered in decision-making processes.

> *"And consult them in the matter. And when you have decided, then rely upon Allah." (Quran 3:159)*

Leading by example, he embodied the values and principles he preached. His actions were consistent with his words, demonstrating integrity and authenticity. This inspired trust and admiration among his followers.

> *"You have indeed in the Messenger of Allah a beautiful pattern [of conduct] for anyone whose hope is in Allah and the Final Day, and who engages much in the praise of Allah." (Quran 33:21)*

Prophet Muhammad's (PBUH) leadership style offers valuable lessons for modern leaders. His principles of compassion, justice, integrity, humility, vision, patience, empowerment, communication, and inclusivity provide a comprehensive framework for effective and ethical leadership.

Importance of applying Sunnah principles in modern business contexts

Sunnah principles are not just historical anecdotes but practical tools that can help navigate today's business challenges with integrity and insight.

One of the key aspects of the Prophet's leadership was his unwavering commitment to ethical behaviour. In today's fast-paced business world, maintaining a strong ethical foundation can be a game-changer. Companies prioritising honesty and transparency naturally build trust with their customers, employees, and stakeholders. This trust isn't just a nice-to-have; it's crucial for long-term success. When a business is known for its ethical practices, it attracts loyal customers and committed employees, creating a stable and trustworthy brand.

Treating employees with respect and kindness is another core principle. Prophet Muhammad (PBUH) always showed immense respect for those who worked with him. Modern businesses that follow this example see significant benefits.

When employees feel valued, they are more engaged, productive, and loyal. Ensuring fair wages, providing safe working conditions, and supporting professional growth are ways to show employees that they matter. This not only boosts morale but also reduces turnover and fosters a positive work environment where innovation and creativity can thrive.

> *"Give the worker his wages before his sweat dries." (Ibn Majah)*

Justice and fairness were integral to the Prophet's approach. Ensuring everyone in the organisation is treated equally promotes a culture of inclusivity and respect. This inclusivity drives engagement and innovation because diverse perspectives lead to better problem-solving and creativity. Businesses that are fair and inclusive attract top talent and foster a collaborative atmosphere, which is essential for success.

Building strong relationships with customers is another area where the Prophet's principles shine. He was known for his ethical dealings and respect for others, setting a high standard for customer relations. Modern businesses can take a page from this book by prioritising customer satisfaction and addressing concerns promptly and fairly. Customers who feel respected and valued are more likely to stay loyal and recommend the business to others.

Social responsibility and community engagement were also key aspects of the Prophet's life. He emphasised the importance of helping others and contributing to the welfare of the community. Businesses today can adopt similar practices by engaging in corporate social responsibility (CSR) activities. This could include supporting local communities, participating in charitable initiatives, or adopting sustainable practices. Not only do these activities enhance the company's reputation, but they also build stronger community ties and contribute to societal well-being.

> *"He is not a believer whose stomach is filled while his neighbour goes hungry." (Al-Adab Al-Mufrad)*

The Prophet's visionary approach to leadership is another principle that modern businesses can adopt. He had a clear vision for the future and communicated it effectively to his followers. Modern business leaders can learn from this by setting clear, long-term goals and ensuring their teams understand and are motivated by these objectives. A well-articulated vision provides direction and purpose, helping align the efforts of the entire organisation towards common goals.

Patience and perseverance were hallmarks of the Prophet's leadership, essential traits for modern business leaders facing the ups and downs of the market. By maintaining patience in the face of setbacks and persevering through difficulties, leaders can inspire their teams to stay focused and motivated, even during challenging times. This resilience is key to navigating the inevitable challenges of business life.

Effective delegation and empowerment are also crucial. The Prophet understood the importance of recognising strengths and entrusting responsibilities to others. Modern leaders can follow this approach by delegating tasks appropriately and fostering a sense of ownership among employees. Empowered employees are more engaged and take greater initiative, driving the organisation towards success.

Clear and transparent communication is vital in any organisation. The Prophet was excellent at conveying his messages clearly, ensuring that his followers were aligned with his vision. In a business context, effective communication helps build trust, avoid misunderstandings, and ensure that all team members are working towards the same goals.

Leading by example is perhaps one of the most powerful principles. The Prophet lived by the values he preached, showing integrity and authenticity in all his actions. Modern leaders who embody the values they expect from their employees set a standard that motivates everyone in the organisation to uphold those values. This kind of leadership inspires trust and respect, essential for a cohesive and successful team.

Applying Sunnah principles in business isn't just following rules; it's creating a culture of trust, respect, and excellence. These principles offer a comprehensive framework for ethical and effective leadership, guiding businesses towards long-term success and positive societal impact. By integrating these timeless values, modern businesses can navigate the complexities of today's world with wisdom and integrity, building strong foundations for the future and making a meaningful difference in their communities.

Relevance of Sunnah Leadership for Muslim Entrepreneurs

Connecting Islamic teachings with contemporary leadership challenges

For Muslim entrepreneurs, integrating the principles of Sunnah into their business practices can offer a unique advantage. Prophet Muhammad (PBUH) left behind a legacy of leadership that emphasised ethics, compassion, and foresight—values that are incredibly relevant in today's business world.

Think about it: in a market where trust is a precious commodity, having a reputation for honesty can set you apart. Transparency in business dealings builds trust with customers and partners alike. When people know they can rely on you to be truthful and fair, they're more likely to stick with you for the long haul. This trust becomes the bedrock of your brand, making your business resilient even when things get tough.

One of Sunnah's core principles is treating employees with respect and kindness. In today's context, this translates to more than just fair pay. It's about creating a work environment where employees feel valued and appreciated. Imagine a workplace where everyone feels like their contributions matter, where professional growth is encouraged, and where work-life balance is respected. When employees feel good about their work environment, they're more engaged and productive. This isn't just good for morale; it's great for business, too.

Fairness and justice are equally crucial. In a diverse and globalised business world, treating all employees and stakeholders with respect regardless of their background is essential. This kind of inclusive culture fosters innovation because people from different backgrounds bring different perspectives and ideas. It's not just about being fair; it's about leveraging diversity to drive creativity and solve problems more effectively.

When it comes to customer relations, the Prophet's example is again spot on. Building strong, ethical relationships with customers can turn them into loyal advocates for your brand. Today's consumers are savvy—they can spot insincerity a mile away. By addressing their needs honestly and fairly, you build a loyal customer base that's not just satisfied but enthusiastic about your business.

Social responsibility is another area where Sunnah principles can make a huge difference. Modern businesses are increasingly expected to play a role in their communities. This isn't just about charity; it's about integrating social good into the core of your business model. Supporting local initiatives, adopting sustainable practices, and ensuring your business decisions positively impact society can build a strong community presence and enhance your brand's reputation.

For instance, consider the emphasis on helping others and benefiting the community, a core teaching in Islam. A business that actively engages in community support and environmental sustainability not only fulfils its ethical obligations but also builds a loyal customer base that values and supports socially responsible businesses. This can be as simple as implementing green policies within the office or sponsoring local events and charities. These actions can foster goodwill and build strong community ties, making the business a respected and integral part of the community.

The importance of having a clear vision and communicating it effectively is another timeless principle. In today's fast-paced business environment, having a long-term strategy that everyone in your organisation understands and buys into is crucial. This vision provides direction and helps align the efforts of your entire team. It's about knowing where you're going and ensuring everyone is on board for the journey.

Patience and perseverance are qualities every entrepreneur needs. The business world is full of ups and downs, and resilience is key to weathering the storms. This means staying committed to your goals even when faced with setbacks. It's about keeping your team motivated and maintaining momentum, no matter what challenges arise.

Delegation and empowerment are also critical. No leader can do everything alone. Recognising the strengths of your team members and trusting them with responsibilities can lead to more effective and efficient business operations. It's about building a team where everyone feels a sense of ownership and is motivated to contribute their best.

Effective communication is vital. The ability to convey your ideas clearly and ensure everyone is on the same page can prevent misunderstandings and keep the business running smoothly. Regular and transparent communication builds team trust and ensures everyone is aligned with the business goals.

Leading by example is perhaps one of the most powerful lessons from the Sunnah. The Prophet's life was a testament to living by the values he preached. For modern entrepreneurs, this means embodying the values you want to see in your business. When you demonstrate integrity, hard work, and dedication, your team is likely to follow suit. This kind of leadership fosters a culture of excellence and respect.

Consider the emphasis on continuous learning and improvement, a significant part of the Prophet's teachings. In a rapidly changing business environment, staying ahead means constantly updating your skills and knowledge. Encouraging a culture of learning within your business can lead to innovation and improvement, keeping your company competitive.

The principle of environmental stewardship is increasingly relevant today. The Prophet emphasised caring for the earth, and modern businesses can integrate this principle by adopting sustainable practices. This isn't just good for the planet; it's good for business. Consumers are increasingly looking for companies that prioritise sustainability, and businesses that do so can enhance their brand image and attract a dedicated customer base.

Emphasising ethical leadership and servant leadership qualities

Ethical leadership is about leading by example with integrity and moral conduct. An ethical leader prioritises honesty, transparency, and justice in all actions and decisions. This leadership style is about following the rules and embodying a strong sense of right and wrong.

Prophet Muhammad (PBUH) was a paragon of ethical leadership. His life provides countless examples of integrity and fairness, setting a benchmark for leaders today.

Ethical leadership fosters a culture of trust within an organisation. When leaders consistently act with integrity, they build credibility and earn the trust of their teams and clients. This trust is the foundation of strong, productive relationships and a positive organisational culture.

Servant Leadership: Serving Others First

Servant leadership, as the name suggests, is about serving others first. This leadership style emphasises the leader's role as a caretaker who prioritises the needs and development of their team members.

Prophet Muhammad (PBUH) exemplified this throughout his life, placing the needs of his companions and followers above his own. He ensured that everyone under his care was treated with kindness and respect, often sacrificing his comfort for the well-being of others.

In modern business, servant leadership can transform how leaders interact with their teams. By focusing on the well-being and growth of employees, leaders can foster a supportive and empowering work environment. This approach enhances job satisfaction and morale, driving higher levels of engagement and productivity.

The Intersection of Ethical and Servant Leadership

While ethical and servant leadership can be viewed as distinct concepts, they intersect significantly. Both styles emphasise values that are essential for building resilient and ethical organisations.

Empathy and Compassion: Both ethical and servant leaders demonstrate empathy and compassion towards others. They listen actively to their team members, understand their needs and concerns, and respond with kindness. This fosters a supportive environment where employees feel valued and respected.

Accountability and Responsibility: Ethical and servant leaders hold themselves accountable for their actions and decisions. They take responsibility for their team's successes and failures, and strive to act in the best interest of their organisation and its stakeholders.

Empowerment and Growth: Servant leadership focuses on empowering team members and supporting their personal and professional growth. Ethical leadership ensures that this empowerment is conducted with integrity and fairness, providing equal opportunities for all.

Building Trust: Trust is a cornerstone of both leadership styles. Ethical leaders build trust through consistent integrity and fairness, while servant leaders build trust by prioritising the needs of their team members. This trust leads to stronger, more cohesive teams and a positive organisational culture.

Practical Applications in Modern Business

In practical terms, implementing these principles in modern business involves several steps. Leading by example is paramount. Leaders must demonstrate integrity, fairness, and empathy in all interactions, modelling the behaviour they expect from their team. This creates a culture of trust and respect.

Open communication is also essential. Leaders should foster an environment where honest dialogue is encouraged, listening actively to their team's concerns and feedback. This not only builds trust but also ensures that everyone feels heard and valued.

Another key aspect is prioritising employee development. Investing in employee growth and development by providing opportunities for learning, mentorship, and career advancement fosters a culture of continuous improvement and engagement.

Creating a supportive environment where the workplace is inclusive and supportive is equally important. Leaders should recognise and address any barriers to employee well-being and success, ensuring that everyone has the opportunity to thrive.

Holding oneself accountable is a crucial aspect of ethical and servant leadership. Leaders must take responsibility for their actions and decisions, admitting mistakes and taking steps to rectify them. This builds a culture of transparency and trust.

Promoting ethical practices within the organisation is also vital. Leaders should establish and enforce ethical standards, ensuring that all business practices align with these principles. This not only fosters a culture of integrity but also ensures long-term sustainability and success.

In essence, the philosophy behind ethical and servant leadership is about building a culture of trust, respect, and continuous improvement. It's about leading with empathy and integrity, prioritising the well-being of others, and fostering an environment where everyone can thrive.

Chapter Two

Integrity and Trustworthiness

In a world where competition is fierce and reputations can be built or shattered in moments, the principles of integrity and trustworthiness stand as the cornerstones of lasting success. In both personal and professional spheres, these values are not merely ideals to aspire to but essential components that define the credibility and reliability of an individual or organisation. The teachings of Prophet Muhammad (PBUH), revered as Al-Amin (the Trustworthy), provide timeless lessons in how integrity and trustworthiness can be practised consistently to build and maintain trust, a quality that is indispensable in today's fast-paced, high-stakes environment.

Prophet Muhammad's (PBUH) reputation for fairness and honesty did not emerge overnight; it was the result of a lifetime of consistent ethical behaviour. Even before he received prophethood, his community recognised him as a man of unshakable integrity. His title, Al-Amin, was a testament to his trustworthiness—a quality that made him a reliable figure in his society. He was often entrusted with valuable goods and sensitive matters because people knew he would handle them with the utmost care and honesty.

This reputation was not built on grand, isolated gestures of morality but on the consistent application of ethical principles in every aspect of life. Whether in business dealings, personal relationships, or communal responsibilities, the Prophet (PBUH) exemplified how trust is earned through consistent, reliable actions and an unwavering commitment to truth and justice. This legacy offers a powerful lesson: integrity is not a switch to be turned on when convenient but a constant state of being that guides every decision and action.

In today's business environment, the stakes are incredibly high. A single ethical lapse can lead to a public scandal, financial loss, and irreversible company reputation damage. In such a climate, integrity and trustworthiness are more critical than ever. Businesses are increasingly held accountable by their shareholders and a wider array of stakeholders, including customers, employees, regulators, and the broader community. The rise of social media and the 24-hour news cycle means that any breach of trust can become global news within minutes, with potentially catastrophic consequences.

For leaders, embodying these values is about avoiding scandal and creating a culture of openness and mutual respect. When leaders act with integrity, they set a standard for everyone in the organisation. Transparency in operations builds confidence among stakeholders, as it shows that the company has nothing to hide and is committed to doing the right thing. Moreover, integrity ensures that decisions are made for the right reasons, fostering an environment where ethical behaviour is the norm rather than the exception.

Building trust within an organisation is not a one-time effort; it requires ongoing dedication and a commitment to consistent, ethical behaviour. Trust is cultivated through clear communication, fulfilling promises, and demonstrating genuine concern for others' well-being. When employees see that their leaders are trustworthy, they are more likely to trust the organisation and its mission. This trust translates into higher levels of employee engagement, loyalty, and productivity.

When leaders consistently communicate openly and honestly with their teams, they create a culture where employees feel valued and respected. This, in turn, leads to a more motivated workforce, as employees are more likely to go above and beyond when they believe in the integrity of their leaders. Furthermore, when leaders fulfil their promises—whether related to promotions, bonuses, or professional development opportunities—they reinforce employees' trust. This trust is crucial in times of change or crisis, as employees are more likely to rally behind leaders they believe are acting in their best interests.

Trustworthiness also extends beyond the internal workings of an organisation. For businesses, building trust with customers is paramount. In a market flooded with choices, customers are more likely to remain loyal to a brand they trust. This trust is built through transparency, consistency, and delivering on promises. Companies that prioritise customer trust not only retain existing customers but also attract new ones through positive word-of-mouth and a strong reputation.

Leadership plays a crucial role in setting the tone for integrity within an organisation. Ethical leaders act as role models, demonstrating through their actions what it means to operate with integrity. This requires a commitment to personal accountability and a willingness to make difficult decisions that align with ethical principles, even when those decisions may not be the most profitable in the short term.

Ethical leadership also involves creating systems and processes that support ethical behaviour throughout the organisation. This might include establishing a code of conduct, implementing training programs on ethical decision-making, and setting up channels for employees to report unethical behaviour without fear of retaliation. By institutionalising ethics, leaders can ensure that integrity and trustworthiness are embedded in the organisation's DNA.

Moreover, ethical leaders understand that their actions have a ripple effect. When leaders demonstrate integrity, they inspire others to do the same. This creates a culture of trust that permeates the entire organisation, leading to stronger relationships, higher employee morale, and a more resilient business.

The true test of integrity and trustworthiness often comes during times of crisis. How leaders respond to challenges—whether a financial downturn, a public relations disaster, or an internal scandal—can define the organisation's reputation for years to come. During such times, the principles of integrity and trustworthiness become even more critical.

Leaders who approach crises with transparency and honesty can mitigate the damage and begin to rebuild trust. This involves acknowledging the issue, taking responsibility, and communicating openly with all stakeholders about the steps to address the situation. By demonstrating integrity in the face of adversity, leaders can turn a crisis into an opportunity to strengthen the organisation's commitment to its core values.

For example, a company that faces a product recall must act swiftly and transparently to protect its customers. By admitting the mistake, recalling the product, and providing clear information about the steps to prevent future issues, the company can maintain customer trust and even enhance its reputation as a responsible and ethical business.

While acting with integrity and trustworthiness may sometimes seem challenging in the short term—especially in a competitive environment where cutting corners might provide a quick advantage—the long-term benefits are undeniable. Companies that prioritise these values build stronger, more resilient organisations better equipped to navigate the complexities of the modern business landscape.

In the long run, integrity and trustworthiness lead to sustainable success. They foster a loyal customer base, attract top talent, and build strong relationships with stakeholders. Moreover, they create a positive organisational culture where employees are proud to work, customers are happy to engage, and partners are eager to collaborate.

Ultimately, integrity and trustworthiness are not just ethical imperatives; they are strategic advantages that can set a company apart in a crowded marketplace. By embodying these principles, leaders can create organisations that are not only successful but also respected and admired for their commitment to doing what is right.

Prophetic Example of Trustworthiness in Business

Importance of honesty, transparency, and integrity in leadership

Prophet Muhammad (PBUH) exemplifies integrity and trustworthiness, especially in his business dealings. His life provides a treasure trove of lessons for modern leaders on the importance of honesty, transparency, and integrity. These values not only uphold ethical standards but also build a foundation for long-term success and trust in business.

Prophet Muhammad (PBUH) was renowned for his integrity long before he received prophethood. His nickname, Al-Amin, meaning "the Trustworthy," was a testament to his impeccable character. This reputation was not built overnight but through consistent actions and a steadfast commitment to honesty and fairness. From a young age, he was known for his truthful and transparent dealings, earning the respect and trust of the people of Mecca.

One profound example of his integrity can be seen in his early business ventures. Before his prophethood, Muhammad (PBUH) worked for Khadijah, a wealthy merchant. Khadijah entrusted him with her trade goods, sending him on business trips due to his reputation for honesty.

On these trips, Muhammad (PBUH) managed the transactions with utmost transparency and ensured that he dealt fairly with all parties involved. His success and fair dealings impressed Khadijah so much that she proposed marriage, highlighting how his trustworthiness built personal and professional bonds. This story is reported in several Islamic texts, including Ibn Ishaq's "Sirat Rasul Allah."

The significance of honesty and integrity in business is multifaceted. First, it builds trust. When leaders are honest and transparent, they earn the trust of their employees, customers, and partners. This trust is foundational for any successful business relationship. People are more likely to engage with and remain loyal to a business they believe operates with integrity. This trust also extends to the broader community, enhancing the business's reputation and attracting more opportunities.

Moreover, honesty and transparency foster a positive organisational culture. When leaders consistently demonstrate these values, they set a standard for the entire organisation. Employees are more likely to emulate these behaviours, creating a culture of integrity. This culture not only enhances internal relationships but also improves overall business performance. Employees who work in an environment of trust and honesty are more engaged and motivated, leading to higher productivity and innovation.

Another insightful example from the Prophet's life is how he handled the trust of others even in challenging situations. During the early days of Islam, when the persecution of Muslims in Mecca became intense, Prophet Muhammad (PBUH) and his followers were forced to migrate to Medina. Despite the hostility and danger, the Prophet ensured that any belongings or trusts left with him were returned to their rightful owners. He assigned Ali (may Allah be pleased with him) to stay behind in Mecca and return these trusts before joining the rest of the Muslims in Medina. This action underscores his unwavering commitment to honesty and integrity, even in the face of personal risk. This incident is documented in Ibn Hisham's "Seerah."

In modern business contexts, this level of integrity translates to ethical practices such as honouring contracts, being transparent about business practices, and ensuring accountability at all levels. When a company is transparent about its operations, it builds credibility. For instance, transparent financial reporting allows stakeholders to see the true state of the business, fostering trust and confidence. Similarly, being open about business challenges and how they are addressed shows a commitment to honesty and problem-solving, rather than hiding issues or misleading stakeholders.

Transparency also plays a crucial role in building and maintaining customer trust. In today's digital age, consumers can access vast amounts of information and easily see through dishonest practices. Companies that are transparent about their products, sourcing, and business practices are more likely to gain customer loyalty. This transparency should extend to how customer complaints and feedback are handled. A business that listens to its customers, addresses their concerns honestly, and makes necessary improvements demonstrates a commitment to integrity that can turn even dissatisfied customers into loyal advocates.

The Prophet's (PBUH) honesty in business dealings also extended to fair trade practices. He would weigh and measure goods accurately and ensure that buyers knew exactly what they were purchasing. This principle is particularly relevant today, where ethical consumerism is on the rise. Modern consumers are increasingly looking for brands that uphold ethical standards. Businesses that are honest about their sourcing, production processes, and labour practices can differentiate themselves in a crowded market. This honesty not only attracts ethically-minded consumers but also sets a standard for the industry.

Moreover, the Prophet's commitment to fairness and justice is critical to integrity. He treated everyone, regardless of their status, with fairness and respect. In a business context, this means ensuring that all employees, from entry-level staff to executives, are treated equitably. Fair wages, opportunities for advancement, and a respectful work environment are all manifestations of this principle. Leaders who demonstrate fairness in their decisions and actions create a more inclusive and motivated workforce.

Another example from the Prophet's life is his mediator role and approach to conflict resolution. His integrity shone through in resolving disputes, always striving for justice and fairness. He listened to all parties involved, understood their perspectives, and made just and equitable decisions. This approach is invaluable in today's business environment, where conflicts and disputes are inevitable. Leaders who handle conflicts with integrity, fairness, and transparency can resolve issues more effectively, maintain harmony, and strengthen trust within the organisation. The Prophet's arbitration during the rebuilding of the Kaaba is a prime example of his wisdom in conflict resolution. When the tribes of Mecca were on the brink of conflict over who would place the Black Stone back in its place, the Prophet came up with a solution that satisfied all parties. He suggested placing the Black Stone on a cloth and having the leaders of each tribe hold the edges, allowing them all to participate in its placement. This incident, reported in various hadith collections like Sahih Bukhari, highlights his ability to resolve disputes fairly and peacefully.

The Prophet's example also teaches us the importance of humility and admitting mistakes. Despite his revered status, he was humble and open to feedback. In the business world, this translates to leaders willing to admit their mistakes, learn from them, and take corrective action. This humility builds a culture of continuous improvement and learning, where employees feel safe to innovate and take risks, knowing that mistakes are part of the growth process.

Prophet Muhammad's (PBUH) life also highlights the importance of trust in leadership. His followers trusted him immensely because they knew he always acted with integrity. In a business context, leaders who consistently demonstrate honesty and integrity inspire trust and loyalty among their teams. This trust is crucial for effective leadership. When employees trust their leaders, they are more likely to be engaged, motivated, and aligned with the organisation's goals.

Trustworthiness in leadership also extends to fulfilling promises and commitments. The Prophet was known for keeping his promises, no matter the cost. This principle is vital in business, where fulfilling commitments to customers, employees, and partners is essential. Leaders who consistently deliver on their promises build a reputation for reliability and integrity, which is invaluable for long-term success.

Furthermore, the Prophet's transparent and honest communication style is a critical aspect of integrity in leadership. He communicated openly with his followers, providing clear guidance and addressing their concerns. In business, transparent communication involves keeping employees informed about the company's direction, challenges, and successes. It means being open about decisions and the reasoning behind them. This transparency fosters a culture of trust and collaboration, where employees feel involved and valued.

Building trust with stakeholders, customers, and team members

Building trust is the cornerstone of any successful business, and it is especially crucial in maintaining long-term relationships with stakeholders, customers, and team members. Trust is not something that can be achieved overnight; it requires consistent effort, transparency, honesty, and integrity. Here, we will delve into how trust can be cultivated and maintained within a business context, drawing lessons from the prophetic example of Prophet Muhammad (PBUH).

Trust with Stakeholders

Stakeholders include investors, business partners, suppliers, and anyone else who has a vested interest in the success of the business. Building trust with stakeholders is critical as it directly impacts the company's reputation, financial health, and strategic growth.

Transparency in Financial Reporting: Prophet Muhammad (PBUH) was known for his clear and honest dealings. In modern business, transparency in financial reporting is paramount. Stakeholders need to know the true financial state of the business to make informed decisions. Regular and accurate financial reports build credibility and foster trust.

Ethical Business Practices: Stakeholders expect the business to operate ethically. This means adhering to laws, following industry standards, and ensuring fair practices. Prophet Muhammad (PBUH) was known for his fairness and justice. Modern businesses can emulate this by ensuring that all dealings are ethical and transparent.

Open Communication: Keeping stakeholders informed about business developments, challenges, and strategic changes is crucial. Regular updates through meetings, reports, and newsletters can keep stakeholders engaged and reassured about their investment. Prophet Muhammad (PBUH) always communicated clearly and effectively, ensuring everyone knew his intentions and actions.

Accountability: Taking responsibility for decisions and actions is a key aspect of trust. When things go wrong, it's important to be upfront, admit mistakes, and take corrective actions. This builds credibility and shows stakeholders that the business is managed with integrity.

Trust with Customers

Customers are the lifeblood of any business. Building trust with customers leads to loyalty, repeat business, and positive word-of-mouth, all of which are essential for long-term success.

Honesty in Advertising: Prophet Muhammad (PBUH) was known for his truthfulness. In modern business, this translates to honesty in advertising and marketing. Misleading customers can lead to loss of trust and legal repercussions. Honest advertising that sets realistic expectations builds a strong, trustworthy brand.

Quality Assurance: Providing consistent quality in products and services is a direct way to build trust. Prophet Muhammad (PBUH) ensured that the goods he traded were of the highest quality. Modern businesses should implement strict quality control measures to ensure that customers receive what they are promised.

Customer Service: Excellent customer service is a hallmark of a trustworthy business. Prompt responses to queries, effective handling of complaints, and a willingness to go the extra mile can significantly enhance customer trust. Prophet Muhammad (PBUH) treated everyone with kindness and respect, and this approach is essential in customer relations today.

Transparency: Being transparent about company policies, pricing, and terms of service helps build trust. Clear and straightforward communication reduces misunderstandings and fosters a sense of security among customers.

Trust with Team Members

Employees are the backbone of any organisation. Building trust with team members leads to higher morale, better performance, and lower turnover rates.

Fair Treatment: Prophet Muhammad (PBUH) was known for his fair treatment of everyone. Modern leaders should ensure that all employees are treated with fairness and respect. This includes fair wages, opportunities for advancement, and recognition of hard work.

Open Communication: Encouraging open communication within the organisation is vital. Employees should feel comfortable sharing their ideas, concerns, and feedback. Regular team meetings and an open-door policy can help foster this environment. The Prophet (PBUH) always listened to his companions, valuing their input and opinions.

Professional Development: Investing in the professional development of employees shows that the organisation values their growth and career progression. Training programs, mentorship, and opportunities for learning can enhance employee satisfaction and loyalty.

Integrity in Leadership: Leaders who demonstrate integrity by consistently acting in line with the organisation's values and principles build trust. Prophet Muhammad (PBUH) led by example, and modern leaders should do the same. This includes being transparent about decisions, admitting mistakes, and always striving to do the right thing.

Recognition and Appreciation: Regularly recognising and appreciating employees' contributions can boost morale and trust. Prophet

Muhammad (PBUH) always acknowledged the efforts of his companions, and this principle is equally important in modern workplaces.

Work-Life Balance: Supporting a healthy work-life balance shows that the organisation cares about the well-being of its employees. Flexible working hours, the option to work remotely, and respecting personal time can help build a supportive and trusting work environment.

Practical Steps to Embrace Honesty, Transparency, and Integrity

Lead by Example: Just as Prophet Muhammad (PBUH) led by personal example, modern leaders should embody honesty, transparency, and integrity in their actions. This sets a standard for the entire organisation.

Communicate Clearly and Openly: Clear and open communication is essential. Leaders should ensure that all stakeholders are well-informed about the organisation's activities, decisions, and challenges. This openness builds trust and prevents misunderstandings.

Establish Ethical Guidelines: Developing and implementing a code of ethics provides clear guidelines for behaviour and decision-making. These guidelines should be communicated to all employees and reinforced through training and regular reminders.

Foster an Open Culture: Encourage a culture where employees feel comfortable raising concerns, asking questions, and providing feedback. This openness helps to identify and address issues before they escalate.

Be Accountable: Leaders should take responsibility for their actions and decisions. Admitting mistakes and taking steps to rectify them demonstrates accountability and integrity.

Ensure Fair Practices: Fairness in dealings with employees, customers, and partners is crucial. This includes fair pricing, transparent contracts, and equitable treatment of all stakeholders.

Regularly Review Practices: Periodic reviews of business practices and policies ensure they align with the principles of honesty, transparency, and integrity. These reviews can help identify areas for improvement and reinforce the organisation's commitment to ethical conduct.

Trust is the bedrock of effective leadership, fostering loyalty, collaboration, and a positive organisational culture. Emulating Prophet Muhammad's (PBUH) approach to business dealings provides a timeless model for building and maintaining trust in all aspects of business.

Upholding Ethical Standards and Values

Aligning business practices with Islamic principles

In today's business world, where ethical missteps can result in significant damage to reputation and finances, maintaining ethical standards and values is crucial. Aligning business practices with Islamic ethics and moral principles not only fulfils religious obligations but also promotes a culture of integrity, transparency, and fairness. These values are universally beneficial and provide a robust framework for ethical business conduct.

Islamic Ethical Principles in Business

Islamic ethics in business revolve around several core principles: justice, honesty, transparency, and accountability. These principles are deeply rooted in the teachings of the Quran and the Sunnah of the Prophet Muhammad (PBUH). By adhering to these principles, businesses can create an environment where ethical behaviour is the norm and not the exception.

Justice and Fairness: Justice is a fundamental tenet of Islamic ethics, requiring fair treatment of all individuals, whether employees, customers, or business partners. This principle ensures equitable practices such as fair pricing, unbiased recruitment processes, and equitable profit-sharing.

> *"Indeed, Allah orders justice and good conduct and giving to relatives and forbids immorality and bad conduct and oppression. He admonishes you that perhaps you will be reminded." (Quran 16:90)*

Prophet Muhammad (PBUH) emphasised justice in all dealings, ensuring everyone received their due rights without discrimination. Modern businesses can emulate this by ensuring that all dealings are ethical and transparent.

Honesty and Truthfulness: Honesty is a cornerstone of Islamic ethics. In business, this means being truthful in all communications, whether in advertising, negotiations, or financial reporting.

> *"And do not mix the truth with falsehood or conceal the truth while you know [it]." (Quran 2:42)*

The Prophet (PBUH) was known for his unwavering honesty, earning him the title "Al-Amin" (the Trustworthy). Modern businesses that prioritise honesty build strong, trusting relationships with stakeholders.

Transparency: Transparency involves being open and clear about business practices, policies, and performance. This principle helps build trust and avoid misunderstandings. Prophet Muhammad (PBUH) practiced transparency in his transactions, ensuring that all parties were fully informed and consented to the terms of trade.

> *"And when you give your word, say the truth [even if a near relative is concerned]; and fulfil the covenant of Allah. This He commands you that you may remember."* (Quran 6:152)

Accountability: Accountability means taking responsibility for one's actions and decisions. In a business context, this involves being answerable to stakeholders and ensuring that all actions are justifiable and in line with ethical standards.

> *"And whatever you spend of expenditures or make of vows - indeed, Allah knows of it. And for the wrongdoers there are no helpers."* (Quran 2:270)

Prophet Muhammad (PBUH) demonstrated accountability by taking responsibility for his actions and decisions, setting a high standard for ethical leadership.

Practical Implementation of Islamic Ethics in Business

Aligning business practices with Islamic ethics requires a strategic approach that incorporates these principles into every aspect of the organisation. Here are some practical steps to achieve this:

Develop a Code of Ethics: Creating a comprehensive code of ethics based on Islamic principles provides clear guidelines for behaviour and decision-making within the organisation. This code should be communicated to all employees and stakeholders to ensure everyone understands and adheres to these standards.

Ethical Training Programs: Implementing training programs focused on Islamic ethics and business principles can help employees understand the importance of ethical behaviour and how to apply these principles in their daily work. Regular workshops and seminars can reinforce these values.

Ethical Leadership: Leaders play a crucial role in setting the ethical tone of an organisation. By demonstrating ethical behaviour, leaders can inspire their teams to follow suit. Ethical leadership involves making decisions that align with Islamic principles, being transparent about business practices, and taking responsibility for actions.

Fair Business Practices: Ensuring fairness in all business operations is vital. This includes fair pricing, transparent contracts, and unbiased treatment of employees and partners. Businesses should strive to create an environment where everyone is treated with respect and equity.

Transparent Financial Reporting: Accurate and transparent financial reporting is essential for building trust with stakeholders. Businesses should ensure that all financial statements are clear, accurate, and provide a true reflection of the company's financial health.

Social Responsibility: Islamic ethics also emphasise the importance of social responsibility. Businesses should engage in practices that benefit society, such as charitable activities, environmentally sustainable practices, and community development projects.

> *"The believers, in their mutual kindness, compassion, and sympathy, are just like one body. When one of the limbs suffers, the whole body responds to it with wakefulness and fever." (Sahih Muslim)*

Prophet Muhammad (PBUH) was a strong advocate for helping others and improving the welfare of the community.

Accountability Mechanisms: Establishing mechanisms for accountability ensures that the organisation remains committed to ethical standards. This can include regular audits, ethical review boards, and transparent reporting channels for misconduct.

Benefits of Aligning with Islamic Ethics

Aligning business practices with Islamic ethics and moral principles offers numerous benefits, including:

Enhanced Reputation: Businesses known for their ethical conduct enjoy a better reputation, which can attract customers, investors, and top talent. A strong ethical reputation differentiates a business in a competitive market.

Increased Trust: Ethical practices build trust among stakeholders. Customers are more likely to remain loyal to a company they trust, and employees are more engaged and motivated when they work for an ethical organisation.

Long-Term Sustainability: Ethical businesses are more likely to achieve long-term success. By making decisions that consider the long-term impact on society and the environment, businesses can ensure their sustainability and continued growth.

Legal Compliance: Adhering to ethical standards helps businesses stay compliant with laws and regulations, reducing the risk of legal issues and fines. Ethical businesses are less likely to engage in practices that could lead to legal trouble.

Positive Work Environment: An ethical workplace fosters a positive environment where employees feel valued and respected. This can lead to higher job satisfaction, increased productivity, and lower turnover rates.

Case Studies of Islamic Ethics in Practice

The Islamic Golden Age: During the Islamic Golden Age, trade and commerce flourished under ethical principles. Traders who adhered to Islamic ethics built strong networks and thriving markets. Their honesty and fairness in dealings attracted traders from different regions, contributing to economic prosperity.

Modern Islamic Finance: The principles of Islamic finance, such as the prohibition of interest (riba) and emphasis on risk-sharing, are rooted in Islamic ethics. Islamic banks and financial institutions operate on ethical principles that promote justice and fairness, providing an alternative to conventional financial systems.

Demonstrating consistency and reliability in decision-making

Consistency in decision-making refers to the uniform application of principles and policies across different situations, while reliability means making decisions that stakeholders can depend on. Together, these qualities form a bedrock of effective leadership and sustainable business practices. This chapter will explore the importance of consistency and reliability in decision-making, how to achieve these qualities, and their impact on organisational success.

The Importance of Consistency and Reliability

Consistency and reliability in decision-making are fundamental for several reasons:

Trust Building: Consistent and reliable decision-making fosters trust among stakeholders, including employees, customers, investors, and partners. When stakeholders see that decisions are made based on clear, consistent principles, they are more likely to trust the leadership.

Predictability: Consistent decision-making provides a sense of predictability, which is comforting in the often-volatile business environment. When employees and other stakeholders understand the criteria and rationale behind decisions, they can anticipate outcomes more accurately.

Fairness: Consistency ensures that decisions are fair and impartial. This helps to avoid perceptions of favouritism or bias, which can undermine morale and trust within the organisation.

Reputation: Organisations known for their reliable decision-making processes often enjoy a stronger reputation. Consistency and reliability signal professionalism and integrity, enhancing the organisation's standing in the market.

Operational Efficiency: Reliable decision-making processes contribute to smoother operations. When decision-making criteria are clear and consistently applied, it reduces confusion and speeds up the decision-making process.

How to Achieve Consistency and Reliability in Decision-Making

Achieving consistency and reliability in decision-making involves several key strategies:

Clear Principles and Values: Establishing a set of clear principles and values that guide decision-making is fundamental. These principles should be rooted in the organisation's mission and ethical standards.

> *"O you who have believed, fear Allah and speak words of appropriate justice." (Quran 33:70)*

Transparent Policies: Developing and communicating transparent policies ensures that everyone in the organisation understands the decision-making framework. Policies should be documented and easily accessible to all stakeholders.

Training and Development: Regular training and development programs help leaders and employees understand and implement the organisation's decision-making processes effectively.

Data-Driven Decisions: Utilising data and analytics can enhance the reliability of decisions. Decisions based on solid data and evidence are more likely to be consistent and reliable.

Feedback Mechanisms: Establishing feedback mechanisms allows for continuous improvement in decision-making processes. Feedback from employees, customers, and other stakeholders can provide valuable insights into the effectiveness of current practices.

Ethical Standards: Upholding high ethical standards in decision-making ensures that decisions are not only consistent but also morally sound. This is particularly important in maintaining the trust and respect of stakeholders.

Documentation and Review: Documenting decisions and the rationale behind them can help ensure consistency over time. Regular reviews of past decisions can also identify patterns and areas for improvement.

Impact of Consistency and Reliability on Organisational Success

The impact of consistent and reliable decision-making on organisational success is profound:

Enhanced Trust and Loyalty: Trust is the foundation of any successful relationship. When stakeholders perceive that decisions are made consistently and reliably, they are more likely to develop loyalty to the organisation. Employees are more engaged and motivated, customers are more loyal, and investors are more confident.

Improved Morale and Engagement: Consistent and fair decision-making boosts employee morale and engagement. When employees understand the decision-making criteria and feel they are applied fairly, they are more likely to be committed to their work and the organisation.

Stronger Reputation: Organisations that demonstrate reliability in their decision-making processes are often seen as more professional and trustworthy. This enhances the organisation's reputation and can attract more customers, investors, and top talent.

Better Risk Management: Consistent decision-making helps in better risk management. When decisions are based on clear principles and reliable data, the organisation is better equipped to anticipate and mitigate risks.

Operational Efficiency: Reliable decision-making processes streamline operations, reducing delays and inefficiencies. This contributes to smoother workflows and higher productivity.

Conflict Resolution: Consistent application of policies and principles helps in resolving conflicts more effectively. When everyone understands and trusts the decision-making framework, it reduces misunderstandings and disputes.

Case Studies and Examples

Prophet Muhammad (PBUH) demonstrated remarkable consistency and reliability in his decision-making. One notable example is the way he handled the distribution of war booty. Despite pressures and potential conflicts, he adhered strictly to the principles of fairness and justice, ensuring that everyone received their due share.

This consistency in upholding justice built immense trust and loyalty among his followers, demonstrating the profound impact of reliable decision-making.

Modern Corporate Practices: Many successful companies today prioritise consistency and reliability in decision-making. For example, tech giants like Google and Apple have clear policies and ethical standards that guide their decisions. Their commitment to data-driven decisions and transparency has contributed significantly to their reputation and success.

Banking and Finance: The Islamic finance industry is built on principles of fairness, transparency, and risk-sharing. Islamic banks consistently apply these principles, ensuring that their financial products and services are ethical and reliable. This consistency has helped the industry gain trust and grow rapidly, even in competitive markets.

Practical Steps for Organisations

Organisations can implement several practical steps to enhance consistency and reliability in decision-making:

Develop a Decision-Making Framework: Create a structured framework that outlines the principles, policies, and processes for decision-making. This framework should be based on the organisation's values and ethical standards.

Train Leaders and Employees: Invest in training programs to ensure that everyone understands the decision-making framework and how to apply it. Regular workshops and refresher courses can reinforce these principles.

Utilise Technology: Leverage technology to support decision-making processes. Tools like data analytics, decision support systems, and project management software can provide valuable insights and enhance consistency.

Encourage Collaboration: Foster a culture of collaboration where diverse perspectives are valued. Collaborative decision-making processes can help ensure that decisions are well-rounded and consider multiple viewpoints.

Monitor and Review: Establish mechanisms to monitor and review decisions regularly. This can help identify inconsistencies and areas for improvement. Feedback loops and performance metrics can provide valuable data for continuous improvement.

Communicate Clearly: Ensure that decisions and the rationale behind them are communicated clearly to all stakeholders. Transparent communication helps build trust and ensures everyone is on the same page.

The examples of Prophet Muhammad (PBUH) and modern successful companies illustrate the profound impact of consistent and reliable decision-making. These qualities not only build trust and loyalty but also contribute to operational efficiency, better risk management, and a stronger reputation. By prioritising consistency and reliability, businesses can navigate the complexities of the modern world with confidence and integrity.

The Intersection of Integrity and Accountability

In leadership and business, two principles often come together to form the foundation of ethical and effective management: integrity and accountability. These principles are not just abstract concepts; they are practical values that leaders must embody to create a trustworthy and successful environment. Integrity refers to honesty and strong moral principles, while accountability means taking responsibility for one's actions and decisions. Combined, these values create a leadership style that inspires trust, motivates teams, and ensures long-term success.

Integrity is about doing the right thing, even when no one is watching. It involves being honest, transparent, and fair in all actions. For leaders, integrity is crucial because it sets the tone for the entire organisation. When leaders demonstrate integrity, they build trust among their employees, customers, and stakeholders.

In the life of Prophet Muhammad (PBUH), integrity was a defining characteristic. He was known as "Al-Amin," "The Trustworthy." His honesty and truthfulness were well-known, and people would entrust him with their belongings and secrets. This trust was not earned overnight; it was built through consistent actions demonstrating his commitment to truth and justice.

One famous incident that highlights the Prophet's integrity occurred before his prophethood, during the rebuilding of the Kaaba. The tribes of Mecca were on the verge of conflict over who would have the honour of placing the Black Stone in its place. The situation was tense, and violence seemed inevitable. The Prophet, who was still a young man, proposed a solution that satisfied all parties. He suggested that the Black Stone be placed on a cloth, and each tribal leader would hold a corner of the cloth, lifting it together to the site.

This fair and wise solution not only prevented bloodshed but also demonstrated the Prophet's integrity in ensuring justice and fairness for all. While integrity is about being honest and fair, accountability is about taking responsibility for one's actions and decisions. A leader who is accountable does not shift blame onto others when things go wrong. Instead, they accept responsibility and work to rectify any mistakes. Accountability is essential for building trust within an organisation because it shows that the leader is committed to the well-being of the team and the success of the organisation.

In the life of Prophet Muhammad (PBUH), we see numerous examples of accountability. The Prophet was always willing to take responsibility for his actions and decisions and encouraged others to do the same. One such example is the Treaty of Hudaybiyyah. This treaty was a pivotal moment in the history of Islam.

The treaty's terms appeared unfavourable to the Muslims at first glance, but the Prophet agreed to avoid conflict and ensure peace. Some of his companions were unhappy with the terms, but the Prophet stood by his decision, showing accountability for the peace process. Over time, the treaty proved beneficial, leading to a period of peace that allowed Islam to spread more effectively.

The Connection Between Integrity and Accountability

Integrity and accountability are deeply interconnected. A leader cannot be truly accountable without integrity, and integrity is meaningless without accountability. Together, they create a leadership style that is both ethical and effective.

When a leader has integrity, they are more likely to hold themselves accountable. They understand that their actions and decisions have consequences and that they must answer for them. This understanding leads to more thoughtful decision-making and a greater commitment to doing what is right, even when difficult.

Conversely, accountability reinforces integrity. When a leader knows that they will be held responsible for their actions, they are more likely to act with integrity. Accountability creates a system of checks and balances that ensures ethical behaviour. It also encourages transparency, as leaders are more likely to be open and honest when they know they will be held accountable.

In a business context, the intersection of integrity and accountability is crucial. Companies that prioritise these values tend to have stronger reputations, more loyal customers, and higher levels of employee engagement. These companies are also better equipped to navigate challenges because their leaders can make tough decisions based on ethical principles, knowing that they will take responsibility for the outcomes.

Prophetic Examples of Integrity and Accountability

The life of Prophet Muhammad (PBUH) is filled with examples where integrity and accountability intersect. These examples provide timeless lessons for modern leaders in both personal and professional settings.

The Incident of the Spoils of War

One of the most telling examples of the Prophet's integrity and accountability occurred during the distribution of the spoils of war after the Battle of Hunayn. The Prophet was responsible for distributing the spoils among his companions and the newly converted Muslims. However, some of the companions felt that the distribution was not fair, and they voiced their concerns.

Instead of dismissing their concerns, the Prophet addressed them openly. He explained his reasons for the distribution and reassured his companions that he was acting in the best interest of the Muslim community.

This incident illustrates how the Prophet combined integrity with accountability by being transparent about his decisions and taking responsibility for them. He did not shy away from criticism but used it to build trust and strengthen the bonds within his community.

The Trust with Abu Sufyan

Another significant example is the Prophet's handling of the trust given to him by Abu Sufyan, a leader of the Quraysh who was initially an enemy of Islam. During the early years of Islam, when the Prophet and his followers were persecuted, Abu Sufyan entrusted the Prophet with some goods for safekeeping.

Despite the hostility between them, the Prophet honoured this trust. When Abu Sufyan came to reclaim his goods, the Prophet returned them in full, demonstrating his unwavering commitment to integrity.

This act not only showcased the Prophet's integrity but also his accountability. He understood that the trust placed in him was sacred, and he fulfilled his obligation, even though it involved someone who had been his adversary. This incident teaches us that integrity and accountability are not conditional; they must be upheld regardless of the circumstances.

Implementing Integrity and Accountability in Modern Leadership

The examples from the life of the Prophet Muhammad (PBUH) offer valuable lessons for modern leaders. But how can these principles be applied in today's fast-paced and often complex business environment?

Leading by Example

One of the most effective ways to implement integrity and accountability in leadership is by leading by example. Leaders who consistently demonstrate these values set the standard for the entire organisation. When employees see their leaders acting with integrity and taking responsibility for their actions, they are more likely to follow suit.

For example, if a leader admits to a mistake and takes steps to correct it, they encourage a culture of accountability. This openness also builds trust, as employees feel they can be honest about their mistakes without fear of retribution. By fostering an environment where integrity and accountability are valued, leaders can create a more cohesive and motivated team.

Establishing Clear Ethical Guidelines

Another important step is to establish clear ethical guidelines within the organisation. These guidelines should outline the values and principles that the organisation stands for, including the importance of integrity and accountability. By having these guidelines in place, leaders can ensure that everyone in the organisation understands the expectations and knows how to act in a way that aligns with the organisation's values.

These guidelines should be reinforced through regular training and communication. Leaders should also be open to feedback and willing to adjust the guidelines as needed to address any ethical challenges that arise.

Creating a Culture of Transparency

Transparency is a key component of both integrity and accountability. Leaders should strive to create a culture of transparency where information is shared openly and honestly. This includes being transparent about decisions, challenges, and the reasoning behind certain actions.

For example, if a company is facing financial difficulties, a leader with integrity will communicate this openly to the employees, explaining the situation and the steps being taken to address it. This transparency not only builds trust but also encourages employees to contribute to finding solutions, knowing that they are part of the process.

Encouraging Open Communication

Open communication is essential for fostering accountability. Leaders should encourage employees to speak up if they see something against the organisation's values. This can be achieved by creating safe channels for reporting concerns and ensuring that there is no retaliation against those who speak out.

In the life of Prophet Muhammad (PBUH), open communication was a hallmark of his leadership. He would often consult with his companions, seek their advice, and listen to their concerns. This approach not only made his companions feel valued but also ensured that decisions were made with the best possible information and insights.

Holding Regular Accountability Sessions

To reinforce accountability, leaders should hold regular accountability sessions where they review decisions and actions, discuss what went well, and identify areas for improvement. These sessions should be conducted in a constructive manner, focusing on learning and growth rather than blame.

By regularly reflecting on their actions and decisions, leaders can ensure that they are staying true to their values of integrity and accountability. These sessions also provide an opportunity to celebrate successes and acknowledge the efforts of team members who have demonstrated these values.

Building Systems of Accountability

In addition to personal accountability, leaders should also build systems of accountability within the organisation. This might include performance reviews, audits, and other mechanisms that ensure everyone is held to the same standards of integrity and responsibility.

For example, a company might implement a system where all major decisions are reviewed by a committee to ensure they align with the organisation's ethical guidelines. This system not only promotes accountability but also ensures that decisions are made in a way that reflects the organisation's commitment to integrity.

The Impact of Integrity and Accountability on Organisational Success

When leaders prioritise integrity and accountability, the impact on the organisation can be profound. These values create a strong foundation for trust, which is essential for building a cohesive and motivated team. Employees are more likely to be engaged and committed when they know that their leaders are acting with integrity and taking responsibility for their actions.

Moreover, a culture of integrity and accountability can enhance the organisation's reputation. Customers, investors, and other stakeholders are more likely to support a company that demonstrates these values. In today's world, where information is readily available and public scrutiny is high, maintaining a reputation for integrity is more important than ever.

A commitment to integrity and accountability also contributes to long-term success. Organisations that uphold these values are better equipped to navigate challenges, make ethical decisions, and build strong relationships with stakeholders. Over time, this leads to a more sustainable and thriving business.

Chapter Three

Empathy and Compassion

In a world where competition and profit margins often dominate, the qualities of empathy and compassion can appear as rare and undervalued treasures. Yet, these traits are not only valuable but essential for sustainable success and creating a positive work environment. Empathy and compassion in leadership involve understanding and addressing the needs and concerns of both employees and customers, fostering a culture of care, and guiding the organisation with kindness and consideration. Prophet Muhammad (PBUH) exemplified these qualities in his leadership, offering timeless lessons for modern business leaders.

Empathy in leadership begins with a deep understanding of the perspectives and feelings of others. It demands that one take the time to listen and genuinely consider the experiences of employees and customers. This understanding transcends mere sympathy; it requires putting oneself in another's shoes to truly grasp their needs and concerns. When leaders practice empathy, they forge stronger relationships, enhance communication, and cultivate a supportive work environment where individuals feel valued and heard.

Creating a culture of care within an organisation starts with the leader. When leaders demonstrate empathy, it sets a tone of mutual respect and support throughout the organisation. This culture encourages team members to look out for one another, collaborate more effectively, and contribute to a positive workplace atmosphere. An empathetic leader recognises that each team member brings unique strengths and challenges and seeks to create an environment where everyone can thrive.

The prophetic model of compassionate leadership, as exemplified by Prophet Muhammad (PBUH), provides a powerful framework for modern leaders. His life was marked by acts of kindness, mercy, and empathy, both in personal interactions and business dealings. He was known for his ability to resolve conflicts with wisdom and understanding, always aiming to achieve peace and fairness. By following this example, leaders can cultivate a leadership style that not only achieves business goals but also builds a loyal and motivated team.

Embracing Empathy in Leadership

Understanding the needs and concerns of employees and customers

Prophet Muhammad (PBUH) showed great empathy in his interactions, understanding and addressing the needs and concerns of those around him. This approach builds trust and loyalty and makes leadership more effective. Today, leaders who practice empathy can make their workplaces better for employees and more appealing to customers, leading to long-term success.

The Prophetic Example of Empathy

Prophet Muhammad (PBUH) was known for his deep empathy. He listened to people's concerns, addressed their needs, and offered support and guidance. His approach was inclusive, considering the well-being of everyone, no matter their status or background. This example shows modern leaders how empathy can improve leadership.

One story from the life of Prophet Muhammad (PBUH) is his interaction with a young boy who had lost his pet bird. The Prophet noticed the boy's sadness and took the time to sit with him, asking about the bird and showing genuine concern. This simple act of empathy showed the Prophet's ability to connect with individuals personally, understanding their emotions and providing comfort.

> *"There has certainly come to you a Messenger from among yourselves. Grievous to him is what you suffer; [he is] concerned over you and to the believers is kind and merciful." (Quran 9:128)*

This verse highlights the importance of gentleness and empathy in leadership, showing that a compassionate approach can strengthen relationships and maintain unity.

One of the most profound examples of prophetic empathy in a business context is the story of the Prophet's (PBUH) approach to fair trade practices, specifically the incident involving the quality of goods in the market. This example is not only a testament to his ethical leadership but also provides deep insights into how empathy can transform business interactions and create a culture of trust and integrity.

The incident is recorded in Ibn Ishaq's "Sirat Rasul Allah", and it describes a moment when Prophet Muhammad (PBUH) noticed a merchant attempting to sell dates of different qualities mixed together. The Prophet gently but firmly addressed the merchant, advising him to separate the good dates from the bad and display them honestly. He is reported to have said, "He who deceives is not of us." This simple yet powerful interaction offers several layers of insight into the Prophet's empathetic approach to business.

First, this story illustrates the Prophet's acute awareness of the buyer's perspective. By advising the merchant to display his goods honestly, the Prophet was ensuring that buyers could make informed decisions.

This level of empathy is crucial in business because it shows a genuine concern for the well-being of customers. It highlights the importance of transparency and honesty, which are fundamental in building trust. When customers feel they are being treated fairly and respectfully, they are more likely to return and become loyal patrons.

Second, the Prophet's approach to the merchant was neither harsh nor punitive. Instead of reprimanding the merchant publicly or punishing him, the Prophet chose a path of gentle correction and guidance. Addressing unethical behaviour with empathy rather than anger fosters a more positive and constructive environment. It encourages individuals to correct their mistakes and align their practices with ethical standards without fear of humiliation or retribution. This approach can be particularly effective in modern business settings where fostering a culture of continuous improvement and ethical behaviour is essential.

Moreover, this example underscores the importance of leading by example. The Prophet didn't just preach honesty; he demonstrated it in his actions and interactions. By embodying the values he espoused, he set a clear standard for others to follow. This leadership style is incredibly powerful because it builds credibility and trust. When leaders practice what they preach, they inspire others to do the same, creating a ripple effect throughout the organisation. In a business context, leaders who consistently demonstrate integrity and empathy set the tone for the entire company, encouraging a culture of ethical behaviour and mutual respect.

The Prophet's advice to the merchant also reflects a deep understanding of the broader impact of business practices on the community. By ensuring that goods are sold honestly, the Prophet was safeguarding the market's overall integrity and fairness. This concern for the collective well-being over individual profit is a vital lesson for modern businesses. In today's interconnected world, unethical practices by a single company can have far-reaching consequences, damaging the entire industry's reputation and trust. By prioritising ethical practices, businesses not only protect their own interests but also contribute to the overall health and sustainability of their industry.

Understanding Employees' Needs and Concerns

In business, understanding the needs and concerns of employees is essential for creating a supportive and engaging workplace. Employees who feel understood and valued are more likely to be motivated, productive, and loyal to the organisation. Here are key strategies to embrace empathy in leadership by addressing employees' needs and concerns:

Active Listening: One of the best ways to understand employees' needs is through active listening. This means fully concentrating, understanding, responding, and remembering what they say. Leaders should create opportunities for open dialogue, such as regular one-on-one meetings or feedback sessions, where employees can share their thoughts and concerns.

Open Communication: Encouraging open communication helps employees feel comfortable expressing their needs. Leaders should be approachable and willing to listen without judgment. This openness builds trust and makes employees feel that their voices are heard and respected.

Personalised Support: Recognising that each employee is unique is crucial. Leaders should strive to understand the individual circumstances and needs of their team members. Providing personalised support through flexible work arrangements, professional development opportunities, or mental health resources shows empathy and a genuine concern for employees' well-being.

Acknowledging Contributions: Acknowledging and appreciating employees' contributions fosters a sense of value and belonging. Leaders should regularly recognise hard work and achievements, both publicly and privately. This recognition can boost morale and motivate employees to continue performing at their best.

Addressing Work-Life Balance: Understanding the importance of work-life balance is essential for empathetic leadership. Leaders should promote policies that support this balance, such as flexible working hours or remote work options. By considering the personal lives of employees, leaders can reduce stress and increase overall job satisfaction.

Understanding Customers' Needs and Concerns

Just as it's important to understand employees, empathising with customers is crucial for building strong, lasting relationships. Customers who feel understood and valued are more likely to remain loyal and recommend the business to others. Here are key strategies for leaders to embrace empathy in understanding customers' needs and concerns:

Customer Feedback: Actively seeking and valuing customer feedback is a primary way to understand their needs and concerns. Surveys, feedback forms, and direct interactions provide valuable insights into what customers value and where improvements are needed.

Personalised Service: Providing personalised service shows an understanding of individual customer needs. Tailoring products, services, and interactions to meet specific customer preferences shows that the business cares about each customer's unique experience.

Responsive Communication: Quick and responsive communication with customers shows empathy and respect. Whether addressing complaints or inquiries, timely and thoughtful responses help build trust and demonstrate a commitment to customer satisfaction.

Proactive Problem Solving: Anticipating and addressing potential issues before they become significant problems is a proactive way to show empathy. By putting themselves in the customers' shoes, leaders can identify pain points and work to resolve them efficiently.

Building Relationships: Building strong relationships with customers goes beyond transactional interactions. Engaging with customers through loyalty programs, personalised follow-ups, and community-building activities can deepen connections and foster loyalty.

The Impact of Empathy in Leadership

Embracing empathy in leadership, as shown by Prophet Muhammad (PBUH), has significant impacts on both employees and customers. Here are some key benefits:

Increased Employee Engagement and Retention: Employees who feel understood and valued are more likely to be engaged and committed to their work. This leads to higher job satisfaction, reduced turnover, and a more motivated workforce.

Enhanced Customer Loyalty: Customers who feel their needs and concerns are genuinely addressed are more likely to remain loyal and advocate for the business. Empathy-driven customer service can turn satisfied customers into brand ambassadors.

Improved Organisational Culture: A culture of empathy promotes respect, collaboration, and mutual support within the organisation. This positive environment encourages innovation, creativity, and high performance.

Strengthened Trust and Credibility: Leaders who consistently demonstrate empathy build trust and credibility with both employees and customers. This trust is essential for navigating challenges and achieving long-term success.

Greater Conflict Resolution: Empathy allows leaders to understand different perspectives and find common ground, leading to more effective conflict resolution. This approach minimises misunderstandings and fosters a cooperative atmosphere.

Higher Productivity and Efficiency: When employees and customers feel understood and supported, they are more likely to engage fully with the organisation. This increased engagement leads to higher productivity and efficiency.

Implementing Empathy in Leadership

To effectively implement empathy in leadership, consider the following steps:

Lead by Example: Leaders should model empathetic behaviour in their interactions. This sets a standard for the entire organisation and encourages others to follow suit.

Training and Development: Provide training programs that focus on developing empathy and emotional intelligence. These programs can help leaders and employees understand the importance of empathy and how to apply it in their roles.

Regular Check-Ins: Implement regular check-ins with employees and customers to gauge their satisfaction and address any concerns. These check-ins provide opportunities for open dialogue and demonstrate a commitment to understanding and meeting their needs.

Encourage Feedback: Create a culture where feedback is encouraged and valued. This feedback can provide insights into how well the organisation is meeting the needs of employees and customers and identify areas for improvement.

Practice Active Listening: Leaders should practice active listening in all interactions. This means fully focusing on the speaker, understanding their message, and responding thoughtfully. Active listening builds trust and shows genuine interest in others' perspectives.

Fostering a culture of care and support within the organisation

Islamic prophetic leadership provides a powerful framework for fostering such a culture, emphasising the importance of compassion, empathy, and mutual support. By drawing on the teachings of the Quran and the example set by Prophet Muhammad (PBUH), modern leaders can build an environment where every individual feels valued and supported.

The Importance of a Supportive Organisational Culture

A supportive organisational culture is crucial for several reasons. Firstly, it prioritises the physical, mental, and emotional well-being of employees, leading to higher job satisfaction, reduced stress, and better overall health. Secondly, employees who feel supported are more motivated and engaged, resulting in higher productivity and better performance. Additionally, a supportive environment fosters loyalty, reducing turnover rates and retaining top talent. Furthermore, it promotes respect, collaboration, and positivity, making the workplace more enjoyable and conducive to creativity and innovation. Finally, companies known for their supportive cultures attract better talent and build stronger relationships with customers and partners.

Islamic Perspective on a Supportive Culture

Islamic teachings emphasise the importance of compassion, empathy, and mutual support, principles that can be directly applied to creating a supportive organisational culture. Compassion and kindness are central tenets of Islam, with the Quran repeatedly encouraging believers to be kind and merciful.

In an organisational context, this means leaders should treat their employees with kindness and empathy, understanding their needs and challenges. Mutual support is also deeply ingrained in Islamic teachings, encouraging believers to support one another, particularly in times of need.

> *"The believers are but brothers, so make settlement between your brothers. And fear Allah that you may receive mercy." (Quran 49:10)*

This principle can be applied in the workplace by fostering a team-oriented environment where colleagues support each other. Fairness and justice are also central to Islamic ethics, urging leaders to be just and fair in their dealings.

Ensuring fairness in policies and practices helps create a supportive and trustworthy environment.

Strategies to Foster a Culture of Care and Support

Creating a culture of care and support within an organisation requires intentional strategies and consistent effort. Leaders should model the behaviour they wish to see in their teams by demonstrating empathy, kindness, and support, setting a positive tone for everyone. One of the most profound examples comes from Prophet Muhammad (PBUH), whose leadership was marked by these qualities.

One strategy is to encourage open and honest communication at all levels. When employees feel safe to express their thoughts, concerns, and suggestions, a more inclusive and supportive environment is created. The Prophet often consulted his companions and valued their opinions, fostering a culture of mutual respect and open dialogue. This practice not only made his followers feel valued but also contributed to more informed and just decisions. For instance, before the Battle of Badr, the Prophet consulted his companions regarding the strategy, ensuring everyone's voice was heard, and ultimately making a decision that reflected the collective wisdom of the group.

Regularly recognising and rewarding employees for their hard work and contributions is another way to foster a sense of value and belonging. Prophet Muhammad (PBUH) was known for acknowledging and praising his companions' efforts. This recognition made them feel appreciated and motivated to continue their efforts with greater zeal. Modern leaders can adopt this practice by celebrating achievements, both big and small, and showing genuine appreciation for their team's efforts. An example from the Prophet's life includes his praise of Muadh ibn Jabal, a young companion, for his knowledge and leadership, which encouraged Muadh and others to continue striving for excellence.

Providing resources that support employees' well-being, such as mental health programs, wellness initiatives, and flexible working arrangements, demonstrates a genuine concern for their well-being. The Prophet's kindness extended to everyone around him, ensuring their physical and emotional needs were met. For example, he showed immense understanding and empathy towards the psychological state of his companions. Once, a young companion named Zahir was feeling down and insecure about his appearance. The Prophet, seeing this, hugged him from behind in a playful manner and publicly expressed his affection and high regard for Zahir, instantly lifting his spirits and showing how a leader's empathy can positively impact an individual's well-being.

Encouraging team collaboration and support through team-building activities, collaborative projects, and a focus on collective achievements helps foster a supportive environment. The Prophet often encouraged his followers to work together, emphasising the strength found in unity. This is exemplified in how he organised and guided the building of the mosque in Medina, where everyone, including the Prophet himself, participated in the construction, fostering a sense of teamwork and collective accomplishment. This hands-on involvement and collaborative spirit set a powerful example for his followers.

Implementing fair policies and practices that promote equity and justice within the organisation ensures fairness and builds trust. The Prophet's fairness in dealing with disputes is legendary. For example, during the rebuilding of the Kaaba, when different tribes argued over who would place the Black Stone, he suggested a solution that involved all the leaders, ensuring fairness and preventing conflict. Leaders today can implement fair practices by ensuring all policies promote equity and justice, thereby building trust within the organisation.

Supporting employees in achieving a healthy work-life balance by offering flexible working hours, remote work options, and encouraging time off to recharge helps reduce stress and increase job satisfaction. The Prophet recognised the importance of balance in life. He would encourage his followers to take time for rest and worship, alongside their daily work and duties. One such instance was when he advised his companion Abdullah ibn Amr to balance his time between worship, family, and rest, emphasising the importance of not overburdening oneself.

Investing in employees' professional and personal development through training programs, workshops, and mentorship shows that the organisation values their growth and development. Prophet Muhammad (PBUH) was a mentor to his companions, guiding them in their personal and spiritual development. He provided them with the knowledge and skills they needed to lead fulfilling lives and contribute positively to their community. For instance, he sent Mus'ab ibn Umair to Medina before the migration to teach the people about Islam, demonstrating trust in his abilities and supporting his leadership development.

The Role of Leadership in Fostering a Supportive Culture

Leadership plays a crucial role in establishing and maintaining a culture of care and support. Leaders should practice empathetic leadership, which involves understanding and addressing the needs and concerns of employees through active listening, personalised support, and being approachable. The Prophet exemplified this by being accessible to his followers, listening to their concerns, and providing guidance and support. An example of this is when he took the time to listen to the complaints of a poor woman who had lost her child, providing her with comfort and assurance, highlighting his empathetic approach.

Transparency in decision-making builds trust and ensures that employees feel included and respected. The Prophet's transparent and just nature is echoed in the Quran:

> *"And when you judge between people, judge with justice." (Quran 4:58)*

Effective conflict resolution is key to maintaining a supportive culture, with leaders addressing conflicts with fairness and empathy, seeking to understand all perspectives and finding mutually beneficial solutions. The Prophet's ability to resolve conflicts with wisdom and fairness, as seen in the incident of the Black Stone, highlights the importance of empathy and justice in leadership. Continuous improvement is also important, with leaders continually seeking feedback and being willing to adapt and improve policies and practices to better support employees, demonstrating a commitment to creating the best possible work environment.

The Impact of a Supportive Culture

A supportive organisational culture has far-reaching impacts, benefiting both the employees and the organisation as a whole. Employees who feel supported are healthier, happier, and more engaged in their work, leading to higher productivity and better performance. A supportive environment fosters loyalty, reducing turnover rates and retaining valuable talent. Organisations known for their supportive cultures attract top talent and build strong relationships with customers and partners. A positive and supportive environment encourages creativity and innovation, driving the organisation forward.

The impact of a supportive culture extends beyond individual well-being, enhancing overall organisational success and reputation. By following the example of Prophet Muhammad (PBUH) and the teachings of the Quran, leaders can create workplaces that thrive on care and support, leading to long-term success and fulfilment for all members of the organisation.

Prophetic Model of Compassionate Leadership

One of the key aspects of compassionate leadership is empathy—understanding and sharing the feelings of others. Prophet Muhammad (PBUH) showed empathy in various situations, listening to people's concerns and offering comfort and guidance.

The Essence of Compassionate Leadership

> *"The believers, in their mutual kindness, compassion, and sympathy, are just like one body. When one of the limbs suffers, the whole body responds to it with wakefulness and fever." (Sahih Muslim)*

This Hadith highlights the interconnectedness of individuals within a community and the importance of empathy and mutual support.

Kindness and Gentleness: Prophet Muhammad (PBUH) was known for his kindness and gentleness. He treated everyone with respect and care, regardless of their status or background.

> *"Whoever is kind, Allah will be kind to him; therefore, be kind to man on the earth. He who is in heaven will show mercy on you."* (Abu Dawud)

This Hadith emphasises the reciprocal nature of kindness and the importance of treating others with gentleness.

Support and Encouragement: A compassionate leader supports and encourages others, helping them to grow and succeed. Prophet Muhammad (PBUH) motivated his followers, providing them with the guidance and encouragement they needed to achieve their potential.

> *"Make things easy for people and do not make them difficult. Cheer people up and do not drive them away."* (Sahih Bukhari)

This Hadith underscores the importance of creating a supportive and positive environment.

Practical Applications of Compassionate Leadership

The principles of compassionate leadership can be applied in various ways within modern organisations to create a supportive and inclusive environment.

Active Listening: Active listening involves fully concentrating, understanding, and responding to what others are saying. Leaders should create opportunities for open dialogue, encouraging employees to share their thoughts and concerns. This practice builds trust and shows that their voices are valued.

Personalised Support: Recognising that each individual has unique needs and circumstances is crucial. Leaders should strive to understand these needs and provide personalised support, whether through flexible work arrangements, professional development opportunities, or mental health resources.

Encouraging Inclusivity: Compassionate leadership involves creating an inclusive environment where everyone feels valued and respected. Leaders should promote diversity and inclusion, ensuring that all team members have equal opportunities to contribute and succeed.

Fostering a Positive Work Environment: A positive work environment is essential for employee well-being and productivity. Leaders should focus on building a culture of respect, collaboration, and positivity, where employees feel safe and supported.

Fairness and Justice: Ensuring fairness and justice in all dealings is a key aspect of compassionate leadership. Leaders should implement fair policies and practices, treating all employees with equity and respect.

"Allah loves those who are just." (Quran 49:9)

This verse emphasises the importance of justice and fairness in leadership.

Prophetic Examples of Compassionate Leadership

Prophet Muhammad's (PBUH) life provides numerous examples of compassionate leadership. These stories illustrate how his approach can be applied in modern leadership contexts.

Resolving Conflicts with Empathy: One notable example is the way Prophet Muhammad (PBUH) resolved conflicts. He approached disputes with empathy, seeking to understand all perspectives and find equitable solutions. This method minimised misunderstandings and promoted harmony.

> *"The best of you are those who are best in resolving conflicts and disputes." (Tirmidhi)*

This Hadith highlights the value of resolving conflicts with compassion and understanding.

Showing Compassion in Business Interactions: In his business dealings, Prophet Muhammad (PBUH) was known for his honesty and compassion. He treated his business partners and customers with kindness, ensuring fair transactions and building lasting relationships.

> *"May Allah have mercy on a man who is kind when he sells, buys, and demands his due." (Sahih Bukhari)*

This Hadith emphasises the importance of compassion and fairness in business interactions.

Supporting the Vulnerable: Prophet Muhammad (PBUH) showed great compassion towards the vulnerable members of society. He supported orphans, widows, and the poor, advocating for their rights and well-being.

> *"The one who cares for an orphan and me will be together in Paradise like this," he said, holding his two fingers together to illustrate. (Sahih Bukhari)*

This Hadith underscores the importance of supporting the vulnerable and the rewards of compassionate leadership.

Promoting Forgiveness and Mercy: Prophet Muhammad (PBUH) promoted forgiveness and mercy, even in difficult situations. His ability to forgive and show mercy inspired his followers and strengthened their commitment to his leadership.

> *"The merciful are shown mercy by the Merciful. Be merciful on the earth, and you will be shown mercy from above." (Tirmidhi)*

This Hadith highlights the importance of mercy and forgiveness in leadership.

Implementing Compassionate Leadership in Modern Organisations

To implement compassionate leadership effectively, leaders can take several practical steps:

Lead by Example: Leaders should model compassionate behaviour in their interactions. By demonstrating empathy, kindness, and support, they set a standard for the entire organisation.

Encourage Open Communication: Creating an environment where open communication is encouraged helps employees feel comfortable expressing their thoughts and concerns. Leaders should be approachable and willing to listen without judgment.

Provide Training and Development: Offering training programs focused on developing empathy and emotional intelligence can help leaders and employees understand the importance of compassionate leadership and how to apply it.

Recognise and Reward Compassionate Behaviour: Acknowledge and reward acts of compassion and kindness within the organisation. This recognition reinforces the value of compassionate leadership and encourages others to follow suit.

Support Work-Life Balance: Supporting employees in achieving a healthy work-life balance is essential for their well-being. Leaders should promote policies that allow for flexibility and encourage employees to take time off to recharge.

Foster Team Collaboration: Encourage team collaboration and support through team-building activities, collaborative projects, and a focus on collective achievements. This approach fosters a sense of community and mutual support.

Ensure Fairness and Justice: Implement fair policies and practices that promote equity and justice within the organisation. Treating all employees with fairness and respect builds trust and loyalty.

The Impact of Compassionate Leadership

Employees who feel understood and valued are more engaged and motivated, leading to higher productivity and better performance. A compassionate environment fosters loyalty, reducing turnover rates and retaining valuable talent. Organisations known for their compassionate cultures attract top talent and build strong relationships with customers and partners. Additionally, a positive and supportive environment encourages creativity and innovation, driving the organisation forward.

The teachings of the Quran and the example set by Prophet Muhammad (PBUH) provide a timeless framework for compassionate leadership, demonstrating that true leadership is about caring for others and striving for the collective good.

Resolving conflicts and addressing challenges with empathy

In any organisation, conflicts and challenges are inevitable. How these are managed can significantly impact the overall health and success of the organisation. Resolving conflicts and addressing challenges with empathy is a hallmark of effective leadership, particularly in the context of Islamic prophetic leadership. Prophet Muhammad (PBUH) set an exemplary standard in handling conflicts and challenges with empathy, providing valuable lessons for modern leaders.

Empathy is the ability to understand and share the feelings of others. It involves considering different perspectives and responding with compassion. In conflict resolution, empathy helps to de-escalate tensions, build trust, and find mutually beneficial solutions. When leaders approach conflicts with empathy, they demonstrate that they value the concerns and feelings of all parties involved.

Prophetic Example of Empathetic Conflict Resolution

Resolving conflicts and addressing challenges with empathy is a cornerstone of effective leadership, and Prophet Muhammad (PBUH) exemplified this approach throughout his life. His methods provide timeless insights into how empathy can transform conflict resolution and turn challenges into opportunities for growth and unity.

One of the most renowned examples of the Prophet's empathetic conflict resolution is the incident during the rebuilding of the Kaaba. The tribes of Mecca were on the brink of violent conflict over the honour of placing the Black Stone in its position. This stone held great religious significance, and each tribe wanted the prestige associated with placing it. Tensions escalated to the point where bloodshed seemed inevitable. However, Prophet Muhammad (PBUH), even before his prophethood, was called upon to mediate the dispute due to his reputation for fairness and wisdom.

Understanding the deep emotions and stakes involved, the Prophet devised a solution that was both simple and profound. He asked for a large cloth to be brought and placed the Black Stone in the centre of it. He then asked a representative from each tribe to hold the edges of the cloth and together lift the stone to its position. Finally, he himself guided the stone into place. This ingenious solution not only averted a potential crisis but also ensured that each tribe felt honoured and included in the process.

The insights drawn from this incident are manifold:

Empathy and Inclusion: The Prophet's approach highlighted the importance of understanding and valuing the perspectives of all parties involved. By devising a solution that included everyone, he ensured that no tribe felt marginalised or disrespected. In a modern business context, leaders can apply this principle by ensuring that all stakeholders are heard and their concerns addressed. This fosters a sense of belonging and mutual respect, which is crucial for maintaining harmony and collaboration within an organisation.

Creative Problem-Solving: The Prophet's solution was innovative and demonstrated his ability to think outside the box. Effective conflict resolution often requires creativity and seeing beyond the obvious solutions. Leaders who approach challenges with an open mind and a willingness to explore unconventional solutions can transform potential conflicts into opportunities for collaboration and growth.

Fairness and Justice: The Prophet's decision was deeply rooted in fairness. He didn't favour any tribe but found a way to give all parties an equal share in the honour. This fairness is essential in any conflict resolution process. Leaders must strive to be impartial and ensure that their decisions are just and equitable, fostering trust and respect among their teams.

Calm and Composure: The Prophet's calm and composed demeanour during the crisis was crucial in de-escalating the situation. Leaders who remain calm under pressure can think more clearly and make better decisions. This calmness also helps to reassure and steady those involved in the conflict, reducing anxiety and tension.

Another significant example of the Prophet's empathetic leadership is his interaction with the Bedouin who urinated in the mosque. The companions of the Prophet reacted with anger and wanted to punish the man. However, the Prophet instructed them to let the Bedouin finish and then gently explained to him the sanctity of the mosque. He personally oversaw the cleaning of the area and advised his companions to be patient and understanding. This incident, recorded in Sahih Bukhari, underscores several key aspects of empathetic conflict resolution:

Patience and Understanding: The Prophet's patience and understanding prevented the situation from escalating. He recognised that the Bedouin's actions were born out of ignorance rather than malice and chose to educate rather than punish him. Modern leaders can learn from this by taking the time to understand the root causes of conflicts and addressing them with patience and empathy.

Educational Approach: The Prophet used the incident as a teaching moment, not just for the Bedouin but for his companions as well. He demonstrated that conflicts could be opportunities for learning and growth. In a business setting, leaders can use conflicts to educate their teams, improve processes, and build a more inclusive and understanding culture.

Leading by Example: By personally overseeing the cleaning of the mosque, the Prophet demonstrated humility and a hands-on approach. Leaders who lead by example and show a willingness to get involved in resolving conflicts directly can inspire their teams and build a culture of mutual respect and cooperation.

Balancing Firmness with Compassion: While the Prophet was firm in explaining the importance of the mosque's sanctity, he did so with compassion and kindness. Effective conflict resolution often requires a balance of firmness and empathy, ensuring that boundaries are respected while also addressing the emotional needs of those involved.

These examples from the Prophet's life illustrate that empathy in conflict resolution is not about avoiding difficult conversations or decisions. Rather, it is about approaching these challenges with a deep understanding of the emotions and perspectives of all parties involved. It involves active listening, creative problem-solving, and a commitment to fairness and justice.

Strategies for Empathetic Conflict Resolution

Encouraging Open Dialogue: Creating an environment where open dialogue is encouraged helps individuals feel comfortable expressing their concerns. Leaders should facilitate discussions where all parties can speak freely without fear of retribution. This openness fosters trust and facilitates honest communication.

Recognising Emotional Triggers: Understanding and recognising emotional triggers can prevent conflicts from escalating. Leaders should be attuned to the emotional states of their team members and address these triggers compassionately. This approach helps calm tensions and promote a more rational discussion.

Providing a Mediation Process: Establishing a formal mediation process can help in resolving conflicts impartially. A mediator, who is neutral and trained in conflict resolution, can facilitate discussions between conflicting parties, ensuring that all perspectives are considered and respected.

Offering Constructive Feedback: When conflicts arise, offering constructive feedback rather than criticism helps to address issues without creating further animosity. Leaders should focus on behaviours and outcomes rather than personal attributes, guiding individuals toward improvement and resolution.

Encouraging Mutual Respect: Promoting a culture of mutual respect within the organisation is essential. Leaders should model respectful behaviour and expect the same from their team. This respect helps in managing conflicts constructively, as all parties are more likely to listen and understand each other.

Seeking Common Ground: In conflict resolution, finding common ground is key. Leaders should identify shared goals and values that can unite conflicting parties. This focus on commonalities rather than differences helps in crafting solutions that are acceptable to all.

Addressing Challenges with Empathy: Just as empathy is vital in conflict resolution, it is equally important in addressing broader organisational challenges. Leaders who approach challenges with empathy can better understand the impact of these challenges on their team and develop strategies that support their well-being.

Understanding the Impact on Employees: When addressing organisational challenges, leaders should consider how these issues affect their employees. This involves understanding the emotional and practical implications of the challenge and providing the necessary support. For example, during times of change or uncertainty, leaders can offer reassurance, clear communication, and resources to help employees adapt.

Involving the Team in Problem-Solving: Involving employees in problem-solving processes can enhance their sense of ownership and engagement. Leaders should encourage team members to share their ideas and suggestions for addressing challenges. This collaborative approach not only generates diverse solutions but also fosters a sense of unity and shared purpose.

Providing Support and Resources: Empathetic leaders ensure that their team has the support and resources needed to navigate challenges. This may include additional training, access to mental health resources, or adjustments to workloads. By providing this support, leaders demonstrate their commitment to their employees' well-being.

Maintaining Open Communication: Open communication is essential when addressing challenges. Leaders should keep their team informed about the nature of the challenge, the steps being taken to address it, and any changes that may affect them. Transparent communication builds trust and helps to alleviate anxiety and uncertainty.

Leading by Example: Leaders should model resilience and a positive attitude when facing challenges. By demonstrating how to approach difficulties with empathy and determination, they inspire their team to do the same. This leadership sets the tone for a supportive and proactive organisational culture.

Compassion in Conflict Resolution

In any organisation or community, conflicts are inevitable. People come from different backgrounds, hold varying opinions, and have unique perspectives, all of which can lead to disagreements. How these conflicts are managed can significantly impact the overall harmony and success of the organisation or community. One of the most powerful tools for resolving conflicts is compassion—a quality that involves understanding, empathy, and a genuine concern for the well-being of others. Compassion in conflict resolution is not just about finding a solution to the problem but about ensuring that the process strengthens relationships, builds trust, and fosters a positive environment.

Compassion in conflict resolution means approaching disputes with an open heart and mind. It involves listening to all sides, understanding the emotions and concerns of those involved, and seeking a resolution that considers everyone's needs. This approach is rooted in the belief that conflicts are not just problems to be solved but opportunities to build stronger, more empathetic relationships.

The concept of compassion is deeply embedded in Islamic teachings, and the life of Prophet Muhammad (PBUH) provides numerous examples of how compassion can transform conflicts into moments of growth and unity. The Prophet's approach to conflict resolution was always guided by a deep sense of empathy, mercy, and fairness, ensuring that even in the most challenging situations, the dignity and well-being of all parties were preserved.

The Importance of Compassion in Conflict Resolution

Conflicts, if not handled properly, can lead to resentment, division, and even long-term damage to relationships. On the other hand, when conflicts are addressed with compassion, they can strengthen bonds, increase understanding, and lead to more effective and harmonious relationships. Compassionate conflict resolution is important for several reasons:

Preserving Relationships: When conflicts are resolved with compassion, the focus is on preserving and even strengthening the relationship between the parties involved. Instead of seeing the other person as an adversary, compassion allows us to see them as fellow human beings with their own struggles and perspectives.

Building Trust: Compassionate conflict resolution builds trust because it shows that the leader or mediator is genuinely concerned about the well-being of all parties. This trust is essential for creating an environment where people feel safe to express their opinions and concerns.

Promoting Understanding: Conflicts often arise from misunderstandings. When we approach conflict with compassion, we take the time to understand the other person's point of view. This understanding can dissolve many conflicts before they escalate and can also prevent future misunderstandings.

Fostering a Positive Environment: An environment where conflicts are resolved with compassion is one where people feel valued and respected. This positive environment encourages open communication, collaboration, and innovation, all of which are essential for the success of any organisation or community.

Incidents Where Prophet Muhammad (PBUH) Used Compassion and Empathy in His Affairs

Prophet Muhammad (PBUH) is revered not only for his spiritual guidance but also for his exemplary character, which was marked by profound compassion and empathy. Throughout his life, he demonstrated these qualities in his interactions with others, whether dealing with friends, family, enemies, or even strangers. His ability to understand and share the feelings of others, coupled with his mercy and kindness, set a standard for ethical behaviour that continues to inspire millions around the world. The following incidents highlight how the Prophet (PBUH) consistently used compassion and empathy in his affairs, offering valuable lessons for humanity.

The Incident of Ta'if

One of the most poignant examples of the Prophet's (PBUH) compassion and empathy occurred during his visit to the city of Ta'if. After facing increasing hostility and persecution in Mecca, the Prophet (PBUH) sought refuge and support in Ta'if, hoping that the people there would be more receptive to his message. However, the people of Ta'if not only rejected him but also subjected him to severe abuse. They mocked him, threw stones at him, and drove him out of the city. He was left wounded and bleeding, yet despite the physical and emotional pain, the Prophet's (PBUH) response was one of compassion and forgiveness.

> *When the Angel Jibril (Gabriel) came to him and offered to destroy the city in response to their cruelty, the Prophet (PBUH) declined. Instead, he prayed for their guidance, saying, "O Allah, guide these people, for they do not know." (Muslim)*

This remarkable act of mercy highlights the Prophet's (PBUH) deep empathy and commitment to responding to hostility with kindness and understanding. He saw beyond their actions, recognising that their behaviour stemmed from ignorance, and he chose to pray for their enlightenment rather than seek revenge.

This incident teaches us that true compassion involves looking beyond one's own pain and considering the long-term well-being of others, even those who have wronged us. It also underscores the power of empathy in transforming hostility into an opportunity for spiritual growth and understanding.

The Compassion Towards the Bedouin Who Urinated in the Mosque

Another incident that showcases the Prophet's (PBUH) empathy and compassion occurred when a Bedouin man entered the mosque in Medina and began to urinate. The companions of the Prophet (PBUH) were outraged by this disrespectful act and rushed to stop the man. However, the Prophet (PBUH) intervened, instructing them to let the man finish and then calmly addressing the situation.

After the man had finished, the Prophet (PBUH) gently explained to him the sanctity of the mosque and why it was inappropriate to urinate there. He then instructed his companions to clean the area where the man had urinated.

> *The Prophet (PBUH) said, "You have been sent to make things easy and not to make things difficult." (Bukhari)*

This incident illustrates the Prophet's (PBUH) deep understanding of human nature and his ability to handle potentially volatile situations with calmness and empathy. Rather than reacting with anger, he chose to educate the man in a gentle and compassionate manner. This approach not only prevented the situation from escalating but also left the Bedouin man with a positive impression of the Prophet (PBUH) and his teachings.

The lesson from this incident is that empathy allows us to respond to mistakes with understanding rather than judgment. By putting ourselves in the other person's shoes, we can address issues in a way that fosters learning and growth rather than conflict and resentment.

The Forgiveness of the People of Mecca

One of the most significant examples of the Prophet's (PBUH) compassion and empathy was his forgiveness of the people of Mecca upon the conquest of the city.

For years, the Meccans had persecuted the Prophet (PBUH) and his followers, driving them out of their homes, torturing and killing many, and waging wars against them. When the Prophet (PBUH) finally returned to Mecca with a large army, he had the power to exact revenge for the injustices they had suffered.

However, instead of seeking retribution, the Prophet (PBUH) chose the path of mercy. He gathered the people of Mecca and asked them,

> "What do you think I will do to you?" They replied, "You are a noble brother and the son of a noble brother." The Prophet (PBUH) then said, "I say to you what Yusuf (Joseph) said to his brothers: 'No blame will there be upon you today. Go, for you are free.'" (Ibn Kathir)

This act of forgiveness was unprecedented and left a deep impact on the people of Mecca. Many who had been staunch enemies of Islam embraced the faith, moved by the Prophet's (PBUH) compassion and magnanimity. The Prophet (PBUH) demonstrated that true strength lies in forgiveness and that empathy allows us to transcend our personal grievances for the greater good.

The conquest of Mecca teaches us that empathy and compassion can heal even the deepest wounds and transform enemies into allies. It also shows that leadership is not just about power but about using that power with mercy and understanding.

The Treatment of Prisoners After the Battle of Badr

After the Battle of Badr, the first major battle between the Muslims and the Quraysh, many of the Quraysh were captured as prisoners of war. The companions of the Prophet (PBUH) were divided on how to deal with these prisoners. Some suggested that they should be executed as a warning to others, while others proposed ransoming them to their families.

The Prophet (PBUH), however, displayed his characteristic compassion and empathy. He chose to treat the prisoners with kindness and gave them the option of being released in exchange for teaching ten Muslims how to read and write. This act not only showed mercy but also highlighted the importance of education and knowledge in Islam.

> *The Prophet (PBUH) instructed his companions to treat the prisoners well, saying, "Feed them from what you eat, and clothe them from what you wear." (Muslim)*

This compassionate treatment of prisoners, who had just been on the battlefield fighting against the Muslims, was unheard of at the time and left a lasting impression on both the prisoners and the Muslim community.

Many prisoners, touched by the Prophet's (PBUH) kindness, eventually embraced Islam. This incident illustrates that empathy and compassion, even in times of conflict, can lead to positive outcomes and win over the hearts of others.

The lesson from this incident is that compassion in dealing with others, especially those who may be considered adversaries, can transform situations and build bridges of understanding and peace.

The Mercy Shown to Hypocrites and Enemies

The Prophet Muhammad (PBUH) also demonstrated compassion and empathy in his dealings with the hypocrites (Munafiqeen) within the Muslim community and with his external enemies. Despite the harm and deceit they caused, the Prophet (PBUH) consistently responded with patience and mercy.

One example is Abdullah ibn Ubayy, the leader of the hypocrites in Medina. Abdullah ibn Ubayy caused significant harm to the Muslim community through his actions, including spreading false rumours about the Prophet's (PBUH) wife, Aisha (RA). Despite these betrayals, the Prophet (PBUH) did not punish him harshly. When Abdullah ibn Ubayy died, the Prophet (PBUH) even prayed for him, though Allah later revealed that such prayers were not to be made for hypocrites.

This incident highlights the Prophet's (PBUH) deep empathy, even for those who opposed him. He always hoped for the best outcome, even for his most treacherous enemies, and sought to guide them rather than punish them harshly.

The lesson here is that compassion and empathy are not reserved only for friends or allies but should extend even to those who oppose or harm us. This approach fosters an environment of forgiveness and healing, rather than one of perpetual conflict and enmity.

The Compassionate Treatment of Children

The Prophet Muhammad (PBUH) was known for his deep love and compassion for children. He treated them with kindness, gentleness, and respect, setting an example for how children should be cared for and nurtured. His interactions with children were marked by empathy and an understanding of their needs and emotions.

One day, while the Prophet (PBUH) was delivering a sermon, he noticed his grandsons, Hasan and Husayn, entering the mosque. They were wearing red shirts and stumbling as they walked. The Prophet (PBUH) could not resist the sight of his beloved grandsons and interrupted his sermon to pick them up. He placed them on his lap and continued his sermon.

> *He then said, "Allah has spoken the truth when He says that your wealth and your children are but a trial. I could not bear to see them stumbling without helping them." (Ibn Majah)*

This incident shows the Prophet's (PBUH) deep empathy for children and his willingness to prioritise their needs, even in the middle of important tasks. His actions demonstrated that children are to be cherished and treated with the utmost care and love.

Another example of the Prophet's (PBUH) compassion towards children is his interaction with Anas ibn Malik, a young boy who served him for ten years.

> *Anas later recalled, "I served the Prophet (PBUH) for ten years, and he never said to me, 'Shame on you' or 'Why did you do such-and-such?' or 'Why did you not do such-and-such?'" (Muslim)*

This remarkable patience and understanding show the Prophet's (PBUH) empathy for the mistakes and limitations of children.

The lesson from these examples is that empathy in dealing with children fosters their growth, confidence, and well-being. It also teaches us to approach children with patience and kindness, recognising their unique needs and feelings.

Compassion for Animals

The Prophet Muhammad (PBUH) also showed great empathy and compassion towards animals, emphasising the importance of treating them with kindness and respect. He taught that animals are part of Allah's creation and should be cared for and protected.

One famous hadith relates that the Prophet (PBUH) saw a camel that was malnourished and overburdened. He approached the owner of the camel and said,

> *"Fear Allah regarding these animals who cannot speak. Ride them while they are healthy, and feed them while they are healthy." (Abu Dawood)*

This incident highlights the Prophet's (PBUH) concern for the well-being of animals and his insistence on their proper care.

In another instance, the Prophet (PBUH) told the story of a woman who was punished by Allah for mistreating a cat. She had kept the cat locked up, denying it food and water, until it died. The Prophet (PBUH) warned that such cruelty would not go unnoticed by Allah and that people would be held accountable for how they treat animals.

The lesson from these incidents is that empathy and compassion extend to all living beings. The Prophet (PBUH) taught that kindness to animals is a reflection of one's character and that even the smallest acts of mercy can have great significance.

The life of Prophet Muhammad (PBUH) is a testament to the power of compassion and empathy in all aspects of life. His ability to understand and share the feelings of others, coupled with his deep concern for their well-being, set a standard for ethical and humane behaviour that continues to inspire people of all faiths.

Whether dealing with enemies, children, animals, or those who wronged him, the Prophet (PBUH) consistently responded with kindness, patience, and understanding. His actions teach us that empathy is not just a feeling but a powerful tool for building stronger, more harmonious relationships and communities.

In today's world, where conflicts and misunderstandings are all too common, the lessons of the Prophet's (PBUH) compassion and empathy are more relevant than ever. Following his example, we can create a more just, peaceful, and compassionate society for all.

Chapter Four

Visionary Leadership and Strategic Planning

Visionary leaders are those who possess the ability to craft a compelling vision for the future, one that aligns with the core values and principles of their organisation. These leaders not only envision where they want their business to go but also inspire and motivate their teams to embark on this journey with enthusiasm and commitment. The power of a clear, well-communicated vision cannot be overstated; it serves as a guiding star, providing direction and purpose to every organisation member.

The life of the Prophet (PBUH) offers profound insights into visionary leadership. His vision was not merely for his time but for generations to come. He envisioned a society based on justice, compassion, and equality, and his strategic actions were meticulously planned to achieve this vision. His ability to inspire his followers, communicate his vision effectively, and remain steadfast in his mission amidst numerous challenges is a testament to his extraordinary leadership.

Communicating this vision effectively is equally important. Leaders must ensure their teams understand and embrace the vision, seeing themselves as integral to its realisation. This involves transparent communication, regular reinforcement of the vision, and creating an environment where every team member feels valued and motivated to contribute.

Developing a Clear Vision for Business Success

Setting goals and objectives inspired by Islamic values and principles

Setting goals and objectives is a foundational step in developing a clear vision for any business. These goals serve as milestones for achieving the broader vision and provide a concrete framework for measuring progress. When these goals are inspired by Islamic values, they reflect a commitment to ethical behaviour, social responsibility, and holistic success.

Tawhid, the concept of the oneness of Allah, is central to Islamic belief and provides a profound basis for setting business goals. This principle encourages leaders to see their business activities as part of a larger purpose, aligning their efforts with the divine will. Goals set with this mindset are not merely about profit but also about contributing to the well-being of society and fulfilling one's responsibilities as a steward of Allah's creation.

> *"Say, 'Indeed, my prayer, my rites of sacrifice, my living and my dying are for Allah, Lord of the worlds.'" (Quran 6:162)*

This verse reminds leaders that all actions, including business activities, should be oriented towards serving Allah and, by extension, serving humanity.

Prophet Muhammad (PBUH) had an extraordinary ability to see the bigger picture. His mission went beyond spreading the message of Islam; it was about building a just, compassionate, and inclusive society. This vision was deeply rooted in Tawhid, reflecting the unity and sovereignty of Allah. His actions were not just about immediate success but about aligning every endeavour with a divine purpose. This kind of holistic vision is essential for modern business leaders. It means setting goals that are not just about profits but about creating a meaningful impact on society and the environment.

One of the most striking examples of the Prophet's visionary leadership is his establishment of the Muslim community in Medina. When he migrated to Medina, he didn't just aim to spread his message; he sought to create a cohesive, well-functioning society. The Charter of Medina, which he established, laid down the rights and responsibilities of all citizens, regardless of their faith. This visionary document emphasised justice, mutual respect, and community welfare. It was a clear articulation of a vision that was inclusive and forward-thinking.

In a business context, this means setting goals that benefit not just the company but also its employees, customers, and the wider community. For instance, a business might aim to reduce its environmental footprint, support community development projects, or ensure fair trade practices. These goals reflect a commitment to the principles of Tawhid, acknowledging that business success is intertwined with the well-being of the community and the environment.

The Prophet's ability to communicate his vision effectively was another critical factor in his success. He ensured that his followers understood and were motivated by the shared goals. This communication was not just about words but about actions that demonstrated his commitment to the vision. In modern business, leaders must similarly ensure that their vision is clearly communicated and that their actions consistently reflect their stated goals. This builds trust and ensures everyone is aligned and working towards the same objectives.

The Prophet's strategic vision also involved meticulous planning and clear objectives. When he established the Charter of Medina, he set out specific guidelines for governance, social justice, and mutual support among the diverse inhabitants of the city. This charter was a visionary document that laid the foundation for a cohesive and inclusive society. For modern business leaders, this translates to the importance of having a clear strategic plan. Setting specific, measurable objectives helps in charting a clear path towards achieving the broader vision. It ensures that every action taken is purposeful and aligned with the overarching goals.

Furthermore, the concept of Tawhid underscores the unity of purpose and action. For Prophet Muhammad (PBUH), this meant that every aspect of his leadership was interconnected and driven by the same divine principles. He did not compartmentalise his roles but integrated them seamlessly, whether leading in battle, teaching, or managing community affairs. This integrated approach is crucial for modern leaders. It means that ethical considerations should be woven into every aspect of business operations, from decision-making processes to everyday interactions with employees and customers. It's about creating a cohesive organisational culture where values and actions are aligned.

An essential part of the prophetic vision was resilience and adaptability. The Prophet faced numerous challenges and setbacks, yet his commitment to his vision remained unwavering. He adapted his strategies as needed but never compromised on his core principles. This resilience is particularly relevant in today's fast-paced business environment, where leaders must navigate constant changes and uncertainties. By maintaining a clear vision and being adaptable in their strategies, leaders can guide their organisations through challenges while staying true to their values.

The role of Tawhid in goal setting also involves accountability and continuous improvement. The Prophet's life was marked by a continuous striving for excellence and seeking Allah's pleasure in all actions. He emphasised the importance of accountability, not just to the community but ultimately to Allah. This sense of accountability drives leaders to set high standards and continuously seek ways to improve. It means regularly evaluating business practices, seeking feedback, and being willing to make necessary changes to better align with ethical standards and the overarching vision.

One of the profound insights from the Prophet's leadership is the emphasis on social responsibility. His vision included taking care of the poor, the orphans, and the marginalised, reflecting the Quranic command to support those in need. In a business context, this translates to corporate social responsibility (CSR). It means setting goals that include not just financial performance but also social and environmental contributions. Businesses can engage in activities such as charitable giving, supporting education and healthcare initiatives, and ensuring ethical labour practices. These actions reflect a commitment to the principles of Tawhid, acknowledging that true success is measured by the positive impact on society.

The Prophet's ability to inspire and mobilise his followers was another key aspect of his visionary leadership. He communicated his vision effectively, ensuring that his followers understood and were motivated. This involved not just verbal communication but also leading by example. He embodied the values he preached, which built trust and inspired others to follow. Modern leaders can learn from this by ensuring that their vision is clearly communicated and consistently demonstrated through their actions. This builds a culture of trust and engagement, where employees feel aligned with the company's goals and are motivated to contribute to its success.

Furthermore, the concept of Tawhid emphasises the importance of seeking knowledge and continuous learning. The Prophet encouraged his followers to seek knowledge, reflecting the Quranic command to learn and understand the world. In a business context, this means fostering a culture of innovation and continuous improvement. It involves investing in employee development, encouraging creative problem-solving, and staying abreast of industry trends and advancements. A commitment to learning ensures that the organisation remains dynamic and capable of adapting to new challenges and opportunities.

Practical Steps for Setting Goals and Objectives

Vision and Mission Statements: A clear vision statement articulates the long-term aspirations of the business, while a mission statement defines the purpose and core values that guide daily operations. Both should be rooted in Islamic principles, reflecting the business's commitment to ethical behaviour, social responsibility, and holistic success.

SMART Goals: Setting SMART goals—Specific, Measurable, Achievable, Relevant, and Time-bound—ensures that objectives are clear and actionable. These goals should align with the broader vision and mission of the business and be inspired by Islamic values.

Stakeholder Engagement: Engaging stakeholders in the goal-setting process ensures that diverse perspectives are considered and that the goals reflect the needs and expectations of all parties involved. This inclusive approach fosters a sense of ownership and commitment to the vision.

Continuous Review and Adaptation: Regularly reviewing and adapting goals is crucial for ensuring they remain relevant and achievable in a changing business environment. This process should include feedback mechanisms to assess progress and make necessary adjustments.

Examples of Goals Inspired by Islamic Values

Ethical Business Practices: A goal might be to ensure all business transactions are conducted with honesty and transparency, reflecting the Islamic principle of integrity.

Social Impact: Another goal could be to allocate a percentage of profits to social causes, such as education or healthcare, in line with the principle of social responsibility.

Environmental Stewardship: Setting objectives to reduce the business's environmental footprint through sustainable practices and resource conservation aligns with the Islamic value of stewardship of the earth.

Employee Well-being: Ensuring fair wages, good working conditions, and opportunities for professional development for all employees reflects the Islamic principle of justice and the importance of caring for one's community.

Communicating vision effectively to inspire and motivate teams

A well-articulated vision provides direction, fosters unity, and drives individuals toward a common goal. Drawing from the life of Prophet Muhammad (PBUH), we can learn valuable lessons about effective communication and leadership. His ability to convey his vision with clarity and passion inspired his followers and established a cohesive and motivated community. Here, we will explore various strategies for communicating vision effectively, supported by examples from the Prophet's life.

Clarity and Simplicity

Effective communication of vision starts with clarity and simplicity. A vision that is easy to understand and remember is more likely to inspire and motivate teams. Prophet Muhammad (PBUH) was known for his clear and concise communication. He used simple language that resonated with his audience, making his message accessible to everyone.

One example of this is the Prophet's (PBUH) teaching of the core tenets of Islam, such as the declaration of faith (Shahada): "There is no god but Allah, and Muhammad is His messenger." This simple yet profound statement encapsulates the essence of Islamic belief and serves as a clear guiding principle for Muslims.

Repetition and Reinforcement

Repetition and reinforcement are essential for ensuring that a vision is internalised by the team. Prophet Muhammad (PBUH) frequently reinforced his messages to ensure they were well-understood and remembered by his followers. He would repeat important teachings and principles during sermons and discussions.

For instance, the Prophet (PBUH) often emphasised the importance of brotherhood and unity among Muslims. He reinforced this vision through various means, including his farewell sermon, where he reiterated key messages about equality, justice, and mutual support. This consistent reinforcement helped solidify these values within the community.

Leading by Example

Leaders who embody the vision they communicate are more likely to inspire their teams. Prophet Muhammad (PBUH) was a living example of the principles he taught. His actions consistently reflected his vision, demonstrating commitment and sincerity.

One notable example is the Prophet's (PBUH) participation in the construction of the mosque in Medina. Despite his leadership position, he actively engaged in carrying bricks and working alongside his followers. This act of humility and dedication inspired his companions to work diligently and fostered a strong sense of solidarity.

Storytelling

Storytelling is a powerful tool for communicating vision. Stories can illustrate abstract concepts, making them more relatable and memorable. Prophet Muhammad (PBUH) frequently used stories and parables to convey his messages.

A significant example is the story of the people of the trench (Ashab al-Ukhdud), which he narrated to teach about the trials and steadfastness in faith. This story not only conveyed the importance of resilience and faith but also inspired his followers to remain steadfast in their beliefs despite challenges.

Personal Engagement

Personal engagement and direct communication can significantly enhance the impact of a vision. Prophet Muhammad (PBUH) often engaged with his followers individually and in small groups, addressing their concerns and encouraging them personally.

One example is his interaction with the young companion, Muadh ibn Jabal. The Prophet (PBUH) personally advised Muadh before sending him to Yemen as a governor, instructing him to prioritise justice and compassion. This personal engagement not only motivated Muadh but also ensured he clearly understood and aligned with the Prophet's vision.

Encouragement and Positive Reinforcement

Encouragement and positive reinforcement are vital for maintaining motivation and commitment to the vision. Prophet Muhammad (PBUH) was known for his encouragement and appreciation of his companions' efforts.

A notable example is his praise for Abu Bakr and Umar for their dedication and support. By publicly acknowledging their contributions, the Prophet (PBUH) reinforced their commitment to the vision and motivated others to strive for similar dedication.

Addressing Concerns and Providing Assurance

Effective communication also involves addressing concerns and providing assurance. Prophet Muhammad (PBUH) was adept at understanding and addressing the fears and anxieties of his followers, providing them with the necessary reassurance to stay committed to the vision.

During the Battle of the Trench, the Muslims faced a formidable coalition of enemies. The Prophet (PBUH) kept his companions motivated by sharing the vision of eventual victory and divine support. His calm and reassuring demeanour helped maintain morale and unity among the Muslims during a challenging time.

Consistent and Transparent Communication

Consistency and transparency in communication build trust and credibility. Prophet Muhammad (PBUH) was known for his honesty and transparency in all his dealings. He communicated openly with his followers, keeping them informed about important matters.

For instance, after the Treaty of Hudaybiyyah, some Muslims were initially disheartened, perceiving it as a disadvantageous agreement. The Prophet (PBUH) explained the strategic significance of the treaty, which eventually led to a period of peace and the spread of Islam. His transparent communication helped the Muslims understand and accept the strategic vision.

Flexibility and Adaptability

While maintaining a clear vision, it is essential to be flexible and adaptable in the approach to achieving it. Prophet Muhammad (PBUH) demonstrated this by adapting his strategies based on circumstances while staying true to the core vision.

An example of this flexibility is the change in the direction of prayer (Qibla). Initially, Muslims prayed towards Jerusalem, but later, the direction was changed to Mecca. This change was communicated effectively and accepted by the Muslim community, demonstrating the Prophet's ability to adapt while maintaining the overall vision.

Building a Sense of Ownership

Fostering a sense of ownership among team members is crucial for the successful implementation of a vision. Prophet Muhammad (PBUH) involved his followers in decision-making processes, making them feel valued and responsible for the collective vision.

During the planning of the Battle of Badr, the Prophet (PBUH) consulted his companions, considering their opinions and insights. This inclusive approach not only enriched the decision-making process but also strengthened the companions' commitment to the cause.

Strategic Planning Based on Sunnah Principles

Utilising strategic thinking and foresight in business planning

Strategic thinking, the art of anticipating future challenges and opportunities while planning accordingly, is essential for effective leadership. It necessitates a profound understanding of the current environment, a clear vision for the future, and the ability to devise innovative solutions.

Foresight, the ability to predict or anticipate future events and trends based on current information and past experiences, complements strategic thinking. Together, these skills enable leaders to navigate uncertainties and guide their organisations toward sustainable success.

Prophet Muhammad (PBUH) exemplified exceptional strategic thinking throughout his leadership. One of the most notable examples is the Treaty of Hudaybiyyah. Initially, many of his followers were disappointed with the treaty's terms, viewing them as unfavourable. However, the Prophet saw the long-term benefits. The treaty allowed Muslims to practice their faith peacefully, which eventually led to the significant spread of Islam. This event is referenced in the Quran:

> *"Indeed, we have given you, [O Muhammad], a clear conquest." (Quran 48:1)*

This verse highlights the strategic importance of the Treaty of Hudaybiyyah and demonstrates the Prophet's exceptional foresight.

Principles of Strategic Planning Based on Sunnah

Shura (Consultation)

Consultation, or Shura, is a fundamental principle in Islamic leadership. Prophet Muhammad (PBUH) regularly consulted with his companions on important matters, valuing their opinions and fostering a sense of collective responsibility. This practice is underscored in the Quran:

> *"And those who have responded to their lord and established prayer and whose affair is [determined by] consultation among themselves, and from what We have provided them, they spend." (Quran 42:38)*

By engaging his companions in decision-making, the Prophet ensured that diverse perspectives were considered, enriching the decisions and building a strong sense of unity and commitment among his followers.

In a modern business context, incorporating Shura means engaging team members and stakeholders in planning. This collaborative approach not only enriches decision-making with diverse viewpoints but also builds trust and commitment to the strategic goals. When employees feel their opinions are valued, they are more likely to be invested in the success of the organisation. This collective responsibility fosters a cohesive work environment where everyone works towards common objectives with a shared sense of purpose.

Tawakkul (Trust in Allah)

While strategic planning involves careful analysis and meticulous preparation, it is equally important to place trust in Allah. Tawakkul, or reliance on Allah, means trusting in Allah's wisdom and guidance while making efforts to achieve one's goals.

This principle emphasises the balance between human effort and divine trust, encouraging leaders to make well-informed decisions while maintaining confidence and composure, knowing that ultimate success is in Allah's hands.

Incorporating Tawakkul in business planning encourages leaders to remain steadfast and optimistic in the face of challenges. It promotes a mindset where meticulous planning is coupled with a serene acceptance of outcomes, fostering resilience and adaptability. Leaders who practice Tawakkul can navigate uncertainties with grace, knowing that their efforts are supported by divine wisdom.

Ethical Conduct

Islamic principles place significant emphasis on ethical conduct in all aspects of life, including business. Prophet Muhammad (PBUH) was renowned for his honesty, fairness, and integrity, earning him the title "Al-Amin" (the Trustworthy). This ethical foundation is crucial for strategic planning, ensuring that all actions are transparent, fair, and aligned with moral values.

In strategic planning, maintaining ethical conduct translates to upholding transparency, fairness, and ethical behaviour. Ethical practices build a positive reputation and ensure long-term sustainability and success. Businesses that prioritise ethics are more likely to earn the trust and loyalty of their customers and stakeholders, fostering a strong, positive brand image.

Long-Term Vision

Prophet Muhammad (PBUH) consistently maintained a long-term perspective in his decisions. His aim was always the enduring success of his mission, rather than short-term gains. This foresight is crucial in strategic planning, where decisions should be made with future implications in mind. Balancing immediate needs with long-term goals ensures that businesses remain resilient and adaptable to changing circumstances.

A clear example of this is the Prophet's planning during the Battle of the Trench (Ghazwa-e-Khandaq). Faced with an imminent threat from a coalition of tribes, the Prophet adopted a defensive strategy by digging a trench around Medina, an idea proposed by his companion Salman Al-Farsi. This innovative approach not only thwarted the enemy's advance but also highlighted the importance of strategic foresight and adaptability.

In a business context, leaders should adopt a long-term vision that balances short-term achievements with sustainable growth. This involves setting goals that not only address immediate challenges but also prepare the organisation for future opportunities and threats. Leaders should continuously evaluate and refine their strategies to ensure they remain aligned with the organisation's long-term objectives.

Prophet Muhammad's (PBUH) strategic thinking was deeply rooted in a philosophy that combined foresight, ethical integrity, and a holistic approach to leadership. His strategies were not just about achieving specific objectives but about creating a framework that would ensure the long-term welfare and prosperity of his community.

This holistic approach is evident in the way he integrated various aspects of life—spiritual, social, economic, and political—into his strategic vision. For instance, his emphasis on economic justice, fair trade, and social welfare programs ensured that the community's growth was inclusive and equitable. His leadership demonstrated that true success is measured not just by material gains but by the overall well-being and harmony of society.

Practical Applications in Business Planning

Market Analysis and Research: Effective strategic planning begins with a thorough understanding of the market. This involves analysing current trends, identifying opportunities and threats, and understanding customer needs. The principle of Shura can be applied here by engaging various stakeholders in the research process and gathering diverse insights to inform decision-making.

Risk Management: Foresight involves anticipating potential risks and developing strategies to mitigate them. This includes financial risks, market volatility, and operational challenges. By incorporating Tawakkul, leaders can approach risk management with confidence, knowing that while they prepare for uncertainties, ultimate control rests with Allah.

Setting Clear Objectives: Clear, specific, and measurable objectives provide direction and a framework for evaluating progress. These objectives should align with the business's long-term vision and ethical values. Regularly reviewing and adjusting these goals ensures that the organisation remains on track.

Resource Allocation: Efficient resource allocation is critical for achieving strategic goals. This involves budgeting, investing in necessary technology and infrastructure, and ensuring that human resources are effectively utilised. Ethical conduct in resource allocation ensures fairness and transparency, fostering a positive organisational culture.

Monitoring and Evaluation: Continuous monitoring and evaluation of strategic initiatives allow businesses to measure progress, identify areas for improvement, and make necessary adjustments. This process should involve regular feedback from stakeholders, aligning with the principle of Shura.

Flexibility and Adaptability: The business environment is dynamic, and strategic plans must be flexible to adapt to changing conditions. Long-term vision provides a stable foundation, while flexibility allows for adjustments in response to new challenges and opportunities. This balance ensures that businesses remain resilient and competitive.

Adapting to changing market conditions while staying true to core values

Core values serve as the foundation of any business. They guide decision-making, shape the company culture, and define the organisation's identity. For businesses rooted in Islamic principles, these values include honesty, fairness, social responsibility, and a commitment to excellence. Adhering to these values builds trust with stakeholders, fosters a positive reputation, and ensures long-term sustainability.

"Indeed, Allah loves those who act justly." (Quran 5:42)

One of the most profound examples of the Prophet's ability to adapt while maintaining core values is the Treaty of Hudaybiyyah. Initially, the terms of the treaty seemed disadvantageous to the Muslims. Many of the Prophet's followers were disappointed and felt that their rights had been compromised. However, the Prophet saw beyond the immediate concessions, recognising the long-term benefits of the treaty. The peace agreement allowed Muslims to practice their faith freely and engage in trade and other social activities without fear of persecution. This period of peace eventually led to the growth and spread of Islam, proving the wisdom of the Prophet's strategic foresight.

This example highlights several critical aspects of adapting to changing conditions while staying true to core values. First, it underscores the importance of long-term vision. The Prophet's decision was guided by his understanding of the broader picture and his unwavering commitment to the mission of spreading Islam. In modern business, this translates to having a clear strategic vision that looks beyond immediate gains. Leaders must be able to see the potential long-term benefits of their decisions and be willing to make short-term sacrifices if necessary.

Second, the Treaty of Hudaybiyyah illustrates the importance of flexibility. The Prophet could adapt his approach to achieve a greater good without compromising his core principles. He demonstrated that flexibility does not mean abandoning values but finding innovative ways to uphold them in changing circumstances. For business leaders, this means being open to new ideas and approaches while ensuring that all actions are aligned with the organisation's core values. Flexibility allows businesses to navigate market shifts and unexpected challenges effectively.

The concept of Shura, or consultation, also played a crucial role in the Prophet's leadership. By consulting with his companions, the Prophet ensured that diverse perspectives were considered, leading to more informed and balanced decisions. This collaborative approach is essential in adapting to market changes. In a business context, leaders should engage their teams and stakeholders in the decision-making process, fostering an environment where diverse viewpoints are valued. This not only enriches the strategic planning process but also builds trust and commitment among team members.

Another significant example from the Prophet's life is his response to the economic challenges faced by the early Muslim community. The economic boycott imposed by the Quraysh in Mecca was a severe test. The Prophet and his followers endured significant hardship, but they remained steadfast and adapted their strategies to survive. They formed stronger internal bonds, supported each other, and relied on their faith to persevere. This resilience and adaptability were crucial in overcoming the boycott.

For modern businesses, this example emphasises the importance of internal strength and unity in the face of external challenges. Building a strong organisational culture where employees support each other and are committed to the company's mission can help businesses navigate tough times. It also highlights the value of resilience—staying committed to core values even when faced with significant difficulties.

Moreover, the Prophet's adaptability extended to his economic policies in Medina. He promoted fair trade practices, established marketplaces, and encouraged entrepreneurship. He also introduced rules to ensure transparency and fairness in transactions.

These measures helped create a stable and prosperous economy. This adaptability, grounded in core ethical principles, ensured that the economic system was both resilient and just.

Navigating Market Changes with Practical Strategies

Core values serve as the foundation of any business. They guide decision-making, shape the company culture, and define the organisation's identity. For businesses rooted in Islamic principles, these values include honesty, fairness, social responsibility, and a commitment to excellence. Adhering to these values builds trust with stakeholders, fosters a positive reputation, and ensures long-term sustainability.

Flexibility in Strategy

While core values remain constant, business strategies should be flexible. This flexibility allows companies to pivot in response to market changes without losing sight of their foundational principles. Strategic planning should include contingency plans that anticipate potential market shifts and outline how the company will respond while maintaining its values.

Stakeholder Engagement

Engaging stakeholders, including customers, employees, and partners, provides valuable insights into market trends and expectations. Regularly soliciting feedback helps businesses understand evolving needs and preferences, enabling them to adapt their offerings accordingly. This engagement should be conducted transparently and ethically, reinforcing the company's commitment to its core values.

Ethical Decision-Making

In times of change, businesses may face difficult decisions that test their commitment to their values. Leaders should prioritise ethical decision-making, considering the long-term impact of their actions on stakeholders and society. This involves evaluating potential outcomes against the company's core values and choosing paths that uphold these principles.

Social Responsibility

Maintaining a commitment to social responsibility is crucial, even when adapting to market changes. Businesses should continue to prioritise initiatives that benefit the community and the environment. This includes sustainable practices, charitable contributions, and efforts to improve societal well-being. By doing so, companies demonstrate that their core values are integral to their operations, regardless of external pressures.

Continuous Learning and Innovation

Businesses must foster a culture of continuous learning and innovation to stay ahead of market trends. Encouraging employees to develop new skills and stay updated with industry developments ensures that the organisation can respond effectively to changes. Innovation should be pursued in ways that align with the company's values, ensuring that new solutions and approaches are ethical and socially responsible.

Chapter Five

Effective Communication Skills

Effective communication is the heartbeat of any thriving organisation. It's the lifeline that bridges leaders with their teams, aligns visions, and fuels collective ambition. In the world of Islamic prophetic leadership, communication is an art form that embodies clarity, empathy, and purpose.

Think about the Prophet Muhammad (PBUH) and how he spoke. His words were clear, deliberate, and packed with meaning. His speeches weren't just words strung together; they were arrows aimed straight at the heart. Each word was chosen with care, making his messages not only heard but felt. He knew that clarity and purpose in communication could light the way for understanding and a unified vision within a team.

But communication is a two-way street. It's about speaking and listening. The Prophet (PBUH) excelled at this. He listened deeply, with genuine empathy. When people came to him with their troubles, he gave them his full attention, validating their feelings and responding with wisdom. This built a profound trust and connection within the community. In our fast-paced world, taking a moment to truly listen can transform team dynamics, creating a workplace where everyone feels heard and valued.

Inspiring a team goes beyond giving orders—it's about touching their souls. The Prophet (PBUH) knew the power of stories. He used parables and tales to convey deep truths and ignite the spirit of his followers. These stories weren't just lessons but sparks that ignited passion and action. Modern leaders can learn from this, using storytelling to craft a vision that is both engaging and motivating.

Prophet Muhammad's (PBUH) approach to communication teaches us to speak with clarity, listen with empathy, and inspire with purpose. His example is a timeless guide for leaders seeking to build a united and driven team. Through heartfelt and effective communication, leaders can create an environment where everyone is connected, motivated, and working towards a common goal.

Communicating with Clarity and Purpose

Prophetic methods of effective communication

Clarity in Communication

Clarity is crucial to ensure messages are understood as intended. Prophet Muhammad (PBUH) was known for his clear and concise speech, using simple, straightforward language that was easily comprehended by his audience. One of the most notable examples of his clear communication is the Farewell Sermon. Delivered during his final pilgrimage, this sermon encapsulated key Islamic teachings and ethical principles in a manner that was easily comprehensible.

> *"O people, lend me an attentive ear, for I know not whether after this year I shall ever be amongst you again. Therefore, listen to what I am saying to you very carefully and take these words to those who could not be present here today." (Sahih Bukhari)*

In this sermon, he articulated fundamental principles such as the sanctity of life, property, and honour, equality among humans, and the importance of justice and fairness. The clarity and directness of his message ensured that it resonated deeply with his audience and was easily transmitted to others.

Purposeful Communication

Communicating with purpose involves having a clear objective and ensuring every interaction is meaningful and directed towards achieving that goal. The Prophet (PBUH) always communicated with a clear purpose, whether it was to teach, guide, resolve conflicts, or inspire.

The Treaty of Hudaybiyyah is an excellent example of his purposeful communication. Despite initial resistance from his followers, Prophet Muhammad (PBUH) communicated the long-term strategic benefits of the treaty. His purposeful communication helped his followers understand the importance of patience and strategic foresight.

> *"By Allah, it is not that we would question your decision, O Messenger of Allah. We only act for the sake of Allah and His Messenger, and by Allah, He will not lead us astray."* (Sahih Bukhari)

This treaty eventually led to a period of peace and allowed the Muslim community to grow stronger. The Prophet's ability to communicate the strategic importance of the treaty demonstrated his foresight and purpose-driven leadership.

Using Examples and Parables

Prophet Muhammad (PBUH) frequently used examples and parables to explain complex concepts in a relatable and understandable manner. This method not only clarified his messages but also made them memorable. In one Hadith, the Prophet (PBUH) compared a believer to a tree.

> *"The example of a believer is like that of a tree which sheds its leaves and remains standing firm. Similarly, a believer remains firm in his faith and sheds his sins."* (Sahih Bukhari)

This parable effectively illustrates the concept of resilience and repentance, making it easier for people to grasp and remember. By using familiar and relatable imagery, the Prophet ensured that his teachings were accessible and impactful.

Active Listening and Empathy

Effective communication is not just about speaking; it also involves active listening and empathy. Prophet Muhammad (PBUH) was an excellent listener, and he would give his full attention to those speaking to him. This practice not only made his interlocutors feel valued but also helped him understand their concerns better.

One poignant example is the incident with the Bedouin who entered the mosque and began urinating. The companions of the Prophet (PBUH) were about to scold him, but the Prophet (PBUH) told them to let him finish. He then calmly explained to the Bedouin why the mosque should be kept clean and instructed his companions to clean the area.

> *"The Prophet said, 'Let him be and pour a bucket of water over it. You have been sent to make things easy and not to make them difficult.'"* (Sahih Bukhari)

This incident demonstrates the Prophet's patience and ability to communicate effectively without causing embarrassment or anger.

Repetition for Emphasis

Repetition is a powerful tool in communication, used to emphasise important points and ensure they are remembered. Prophet Muhammad (PBUH) often repeated key messages to reinforce their importance. He repeatedly emphasised the significance of prayer, understanding its central role in a Muslim's life.

> *"The Prophet said, 'The first matter that the slave will be brought to account for on the Day of Judgment is the prayer. If it is sound, then the rest of his deeds will be sound. If it is deficient, then the rest of his deeds will be deficient. " (Tirmidhi)*

By frequently discussing the importance of prayer, he ensured that this core aspect of Islamic practice was deeply ingrained in the minds of his followers.

Non-Verbal Communication

Non-verbal communication, such as body language and gestures, also plays a crucial role in effective communication. Prophet Muhammad (PBUH) used non-verbal cues to reinforce his messages and connect with his audience. His smile, for example, was a powerful non-verbal communication tool. He often used it to convey warmth, kindness, and empathy, making people feel welcome and valued.

> *"I have never seen a man who smiled as much as the Messenger of Allah." (Shama'il al-Muhammadiyah)*

His smile made him approachable and helped to create a positive and engaging atmosphere, which is essential for effective communication.

Tailoring the Message to the Audience

Prophet Muhammad (PBUH) was adept at tailoring his messages to suit the understanding and needs of his audience. He would adjust his language and approach based on the listener's background and level of knowledge. When sending Muadh ibn Jabal to Yemen as a governor, the Prophet (PBUH) provided him with tailored advice suited to his new role.

> *"O Muadh, you are going to a people of the Book. First, invite them to testify that none has the right to be worshipped but Allah and that Muhammad is His Messenger. If they obey you in that, tell them that Allah has enjoined upon them five prayers every day and night..."* (Sahih Bukhari)

This tailored guidance ensured that Muadh was well-prepared for his responsibilities and could communicate effectively with the people he would govern.

Inspiring and Motivating Teams

Using storytelling and motivational speeches to inspire action

One of the most powerful ways to inspire and motivate teams is through storytelling and motivational speeches. These techniques have been used by leaders throughout history to convey messages, instil values, and encourage action. Prophet Muhammad (PBUH) was a master of this art, using stories and speeches to inspire his followers and lead them toward greater achievements.

Storytelling goes beyond simply passing on information. It engages emotions, builds connections, and makes messages memorable. Stories can illuminate complex concepts, making them relatable and easier to understand. Prophet Muhammad (PBUH) frequently used stories and parables to convey important lessons.

Consider the story of the three men trapped in a cave. They invoked Allah by recounting their sincere deeds, and with each invocation, the rock blocking their exit moved slightly.

> *"A rock fell on the mouth of a cave and blocked it. They said, 'There is no way for you to get out of this cave except by invoking Allah by giving reference to the righteous deeds which you have done (for Allah's sake only).'" (Sahih Bukhari)*

This story highlights the power of sincere actions and reliance on Allah. It not only imparts a moral lesson but also inspires listeners to reflect on their deeds and strive for righteousness.

Applying Storytelling in Modern Leadership

In today's organisational context, leaders can harness the power of storytelling to:

Communicate Vision and Values: Stories can encapsulate the organisation's vision and core values, making them more tangible and easier to remember. Imagine a leader sharing the tale of the company's humble beginnings, grounded in innovation and integrity. Such a story can inspire employees to uphold these values in their daily work.

Illustrate Success and Overcoming Challenges: Sharing stories of past triumphs and how obstacles were surmounted can motivate teams to stay resilient and optimistic. These narratives serve as reminders that challenges can be overcome through determination and teamwork.

Build Emotional Connections: Stories humanise leaders and foster emotional connections with team members. By sharing personal anecdotes, leaders can show vulnerability and authenticity, cultivating trust and camaraderie.

Encourage Desired Behaviours: Highlighting stories of exemplary behaviour and achievements can serve as models for employees to emulate. Recognising and sharing these stories reinforces desired behaviours and inspires others to follow suit.

The Impact of Motivational Speeches

Motivational speeches have the power to energise, uplift, and mobilise people toward a common goal. Prophet Muhammad (PBUH) delivered many speeches that inspired his followers to take action and remain steadfast in their faith. One of his most famous speeches is the Farewell Sermon. In this address, he emphasised the principles of equality, justice, and brotherhood.

> *"All mankind is from Adam and Eve. An Arab has no superiority over a non-Arab, nor does a non-Arab have any superiority over an Arab; a white has no superiority over a black, nor does a black have any superiority over a white; none have superiority over another except by piety and good action." (Sahih Bukhari)*

This sermon inspired his followers to embrace unity, equality, and righteousness, leaving a lasting impact on the Muslim community.

Delivering Effective Motivational Speeches

Modern leaders can draw from the Prophet's example to deliver impactful motivational speeches by:

Connecting with the Audience: Understanding the audience's needs, concerns, and aspirations is crucial for delivering a resonant speech. Tailoring messages to address these factors makes the speech relevant and meaningful.

Using Powerful Language: The choice of words can significantly affect a speech's impact. Using powerful, positive, and action-oriented language can inspire and motivate the audience. Metaphors, analogies, and rhetorical questions can enhance the speech's effectiveness.

Sharing Personal Stories and Experiences: Personal stories and experiences make speeches more relatable and authentic. Leaders who share their challenges and triumphs can inspire their teams to overcome obstacles and strive for excellence.

Emphasising Core Values and Vision: Reinforcing the organisation's core values and vision helps align the team's efforts towards common goals. Highlighting how these values guide the organisation's actions can inspire the team to embody them in their work.

Encouraging Action and Providing Clear Steps: A motivational speech should not only inspire but also provide clear steps for action. Outlining specific actions that the team can take to achieve their goals makes it easier for them to translate inspiration into tangible results.

Using Non-Verbal Communication: Non-verbal cues such as body language, eye contact, and facial expressions play a crucial role in delivering an effective speech. Confident and positive non-verbal communication can enhance the speech's impact and engage the audience.

Combining Storytelling and Motivational Speeches

When combined, storytelling and motivational speeches create a powerful synergy. Stories illustrate the key points of a speech, making them more vivid and memorable. They provide concrete examples that reinforce the speech's messages.

Imagine a leader addressing their team during a challenging period. The leader might begin with a story about a time when the organisation faced similar challenges and overcame them through resilience and teamwork. This story sets the stage for the motivational speech, which then emphasises the importance of unity, perseverance, and collective effort. By combining storytelling with motivational speech, the leader can effectively inspire the team to stay committed and work together towards overcoming the current challenges.

Prophet Muhammad's (PBUH) use of storytelling and motivational speeches goes beyond mere technique—it's a profound demonstration of his understanding of human nature and the power of words. His stories were not just moral lessons; they were deeply embedded with spiritual insights and practical wisdom. His speeches were not mere exhortations; they were carefully crafted messages aimed at stirring the soul and galvanising action.

The Prophet's ability to connect with his audience on an emotional level is a testament to his empathetic leadership. He understood that people are not just rational beings but emotional ones. By engaging their hearts as well as their minds, he was able to inspire genuine commitment and action.

In a modern business context, leaders who emulate this approach can create a culture of engagement and motivation. By speaking with authenticity, sharing personal and organisational stories, and delivering messages with clarity and purpose, they can inspire their teams to achieve great things.

The Prophet's approach to communication teaches us that effective leadership is about inspiring people, building bridges, fostering trust, and driving collective action. Through storytelling and motivational speeches, leaders can create a shared vision, instil core values, and inspire their teams to reach new heights.

Building rapport and fostering teamwork through communication

Building rapport is essential for creating a positive and productive work environment. Rapport is the foundation of trust and mutual respect between team members and leaders. When people feel connected and understood, they are more likely to collaborate effectively and contribute to the team's goals.

Prophetic Example of Building Rapport

Prophet Muhammad (PBUH) excelled at building rapport with those around him. He treated everyone with kindness and respect, regardless of their status or background. His interactions were characterised by genuine concern and empathy, which helped him build strong, trusting relationships.

One notable example is his relationship with his companions. The Prophet (PBUH) would spend time with them, listen to their concerns, and offer advice. His approachability and genuine interest in their well-being fostered a deep sense of loyalty and camaraderie among his followers.

> *"The Prophet was closer to the believers than their own selves, and his wives are (as) their mothers." (Quran 33:6)*

This verse highlights the close bond the Prophet had with his followers, illustrating the depth of rapport he built through his compassionate and respectful communication.

Prophetic Example of Fostering Teamwork

Prophet Muhammad (PBUH) demonstrated exemplary teamwork during the construction of the mosque in Medina. Despite being the leader, he participated in the labour alongside his companions, setting an example of collaboration and unity.

> *"The Prophet was carrying along with them until it affected his skin. One of the companions said, 'O Prophet of Allah, let us carry that for you.' The Prophet replied, 'You are not stronger than me, and I am in need of reward just as you are.'" (Sahih Bukhari)*

This example shows how the Prophet fostered teamwork by working alongside his followers and demonstrating that every contribution was valuable.

Insights and Application

Building Rapport Through Active Listening

Prophet Muhammad (PBUH) was known for his exceptional listening skills. He would fully engage with those speaking to him, showing them that their words were important. This practice built a strong foundation of trust and respect.

In a modern workplace, leaders can emulate this by being fully present during conversations, acknowledging the speaker's points, and providing thoughtful feedback.

Empathy and Genuine Concern

The Prophet's empathy was evident in his interactions. He understood the struggles of his followers and offered support and guidance. Leaders today can build rapport by showing genuine concern for their team members' well-being, understanding their challenges, and providing the necessary support to help them succeed.

Consistency in Communication

Regular and open communication was a hallmark of the Prophet's leadership. He kept his followers informed and involved, which built a cohesive and united community. Modern leaders can adopt this approach by holding regular meetings, providing updates, and creating platforms for open dialogue, ensuring everyone feels part of the team.

Positive Reinforcement and Recognition

The Prophet was known for acknowledging the efforts of his followers, reinforcing positive behaviour. Recognising and celebrating achievements can boost morale and motivate team members to continue performing at their best. Simple gestures of appreciation, such as verbal praise or public acknowledgements, can go a long way in building a positive work environment.

Fostering Teamwork

Leading by Example

Prophet Muhammad (PBUH) led by example, participating in the work alongside his followers. This not only showed his commitment but also demonstrated the importance of every individual's contribution. Leaders can foster teamwork by being involved and showing that they are willing to work alongside their team members.

Creating a Culture of Collaboration

The Prophet's approach during the construction of the mosque in Medina illustrates how a collaborative effort can lead to great achievements. Leaders can encourage teamwork by creating a culture that values collaboration, where every team member feels their contribution is essential and appreciated.

Encouraging Open Dialogue

Open and respectful communication is key to resolving conflicts and fostering teamwork. By encouraging open dialogue and ensuring that all voices are heard, leaders can create an environment where team members feel comfortable sharing ideas and working together towards common goals.

Building Trust and Unity

The Prophet's ability to build rapport and foster teamwork created a strong, united community. Leaders can achieve similar results by building trust, showing respect, and fostering a sense of unity within their teams. This leads to a more cohesive and effective workforce, capable of achieving organisational goals.

Active Listening: Building Stronger Connections

In our fast-paced world, effective communication is more important than ever. However, communication is not just about speaking or conveying a message; it's equally about listening. The art of listening is a crucial skill that forms the foundation of strong, meaningful connections, whether in personal relationships, professional environments, or community interactions.

By truly listening, we demonstrate respect, empathy, and a genuine interest in others, which are all essential for building trust and fostering positive relationships.

In leadership, the ability to listen effectively is a hallmark of great leaders. It allows them to understand the needs, concerns, and perspectives of others, leading to more informed decision-making and stronger, more cohesive teams. The life of Prophet Muhammad (PBUH) offers profound examples of how active listening can be used to build connections, resolve conflicts, and guide others with wisdom and compassion.

The Importance of Active Listening

Active listening is more than just hearing the words that someone is saying; it involves fully engaging with the speaker, understanding their message, and responding thoughtfully. When we listen actively, we not only process the information being conveyed but also pick up on the speaker's emotions, intentions, and underlying concerns. This deeper level of understanding is what differentiates active listening from passive hearing.

Active listening has several benefits:

Building Trust and Rapport: When people feel heard and understood, they are more likely to trust and connect with the listener. This trust is the foundation of any strong relationship, whether personal or professional.

Improving Problem-Solving: By fully understanding the concerns and perspectives of others, we can approach problems more effectively and find solutions that address the root causes.

Enhancing Emotional Intelligence: Active listening helps us become more attuned to the emotions of others, which is a key component of emotional intelligence. This awareness allows us to respond in ways that are supportive and empathetic.

Preventing Misunderstandings: Many conflicts and misunderstandings arise from a failure to listen properly. By engaging in active listening, we can ensure that we fully understand the message being conveyed, reducing the likelihood of miscommunication.

Strengthening Team Dynamics: In a team setting, active listening fosters a culture of respect and collaboration. When team members feel that their voices are heard, they are more likely to contribute positively and work together effectively.

Techniques for Active Listening

Active listening is a skill that can be developed and refined over time. Here are some techniques that can help improve your ability to listen actively:

Give Your Full Attention: When someone is speaking to you, make a conscious effort to focus entirely on them. This means avoiding distractions, such as checking your phone or letting your mind wander. By giving the speaker your full attention, you show that you value what they have to say.

Use Non-Verbal Cues: Non-verbal communication plays a significant role in active listening. Nodding, maintaining eye contact, and using facial expressions that reflect your engagement can all signal to the speaker that you are actively listening. These cues help to build a connection and encourage the speaker to continue sharing.

Avoid Interrupting: Interrupting the speaker not only disrupts their train of thought but also sends the message that you are more interested in expressing your own views than in understanding theirs. Allow the speaker to finish their thoughts before responding, and resist the urge to interject with your own opinions or solutions.

Ask Clarifying Questions: To ensure that you fully understand the speaker's message, ask questions that clarify their points. For example, you might say, "Can you explain that further?" or "What did you mean by that?" These questions show that you are engaged and seeking a deeper understanding of what they are saying.

Paraphrase and Reflect: Paraphrasing involves restating what the speaker has said in your own words. This technique not only helps you confirm that you have understood the message correctly but also signals to the speaker that you are actively processing their information. For instance, you might say, "So, what you're saying is..." followed by your interpretation of their message.

Empathise with the Speaker: Empathy is a critical component of active listening. Try to put yourself in the speaker's shoes and understand their emotions and perspective. This empathetic approach helps to build a deeper connection and allows you to respond in a way that is supportive and understanding.

Provide Thoughtful Feedback: After listening to the speaker, offer feedback that reflects your understanding and shows that you have been paying attention. This could be as simple as acknowledging their feelings or providing a thoughtful response that addresses their concerns.

Prophetic Examples of Active Listening

The life of Prophet Muhammad (PBUH) provides numerous examples of how active listening can be used to build connections, resolve conflicts, and guide others with wisdom and compassion. His ability to listen deeply and respond thoughtfully was a key aspect of his leadership and a testament to his exceptional character.

Listening to the Concerns of the Oppressed

Prophet Muhammad (PBUH) was known for his deep empathy and concern for the oppressed and marginalised members of society. He would listen attentively to their grievances and take their concerns seriously, regardless of their social status or background. One such example is the case of a poor woman who approached the Prophet (PBUH) with a complaint. Despite his busy schedule, the Prophet

(PBUH) made time to listen to her and addressed her concerns with kindness and fairness.

This incident highlights the Prophet's (PBUH) commitment to listening to those who were often ignored or overlooked by society. His willingness to listen to the concerns of the oppressed not only provided them with a sense of dignity and respect but also reinforced his role as a just and compassionate leader.

The Story of the Bedouin

Another example of the Prophet's (PBUH) active listening skills is the story of a Bedouin who came to the mosque and prayed in a manner that was not in accordance with Islamic teachings. The companions were quick to correct him, but the Prophet (PBUH) gently intervened. He listened to the Bedouin's concerns and then explained the correct way to pray in a manner that was kind and respectful.

This incident demonstrates the Prophet's (PBUH) ability to listen without judgment and to respond with empathy and guidance. Rather than scolding the Bedouin, he took the time to understand his perspective and provided constructive feedback that was both educational and compassionate.

The Treaty of Hudaybiyyah

The Treaty of Hudaybiyyah is another example of how the Prophet's (PBUH) listening skills played a crucial role in resolving conflicts and building stronger connections. During the negotiations for the treaty, the Prophet (PBUH) listened carefully to the demands and concerns of the Quraysh, even when some of his companions were frustrated by the concessions he was willing to make.

By listening to the Quraysh and seeking a peaceful resolution, the Prophet (PBUH) was able to secure a treaty that ultimately benefited the Muslim community. His ability to listen and understand the concerns of his adversaries demonstrated his wisdom and commitment to peace and reconciliation.

The Incident of Ifk (The Slander of Aisha)

One of the most challenging periods in the life of Prophet Muhammad (PBUH) was the incident of Ifk, when false accusations were made against his beloved wife, Aisha (RA). The situation caused great distress within the Muslim community, and many people began to spread rumours.

Throughout this ordeal, the Prophet (PBUH) demonstrated remarkable patience and restraint. He listened carefully to all sides of the story, including Aisha's own account, and refrained from making any hasty judgments. Instead, he sought divine guidance and waited for the truth to be revealed through a revelation from Allah.

This incident illustrates the importance of listening with an open mind and reserving judgment until all the facts are known. The Prophet's (PBUH) approach to this situation prevented further harm and ensured that justice was served, reinforcing the value of active listening in times of conflict and uncertainty.

Listening to Children

Prophet Muhammad (PBUH) also demonstrated exceptional listening skills in his interactions with children. He treated them with the same respect and attention that he gave to adults, understanding that listening to children was key to nurturing their growth and development.

Anas ibn Malik, who served the Prophet (PBUH) during his youth, recounted how the Prophet (PBUH) would listen patiently to him and other children, never dismissing their concerns or treating them as unimportant. This approach not only strengthened the bond between the Prophet (PBUH) and the children but also taught them the importance of empathy and respect in their own interactions.

The lesson from these examples is that active listening is a powerful tool for building trust, fostering understanding, and guiding others with wisdom and compassion. Whether in personal relationships, professional settings, or broader community interactions, the ability to listen deeply and respond thoughtfully is essential for effective communication and leadership.

Applying Active Listening in Modern Leadership

The examples from the life of the Prophet Muhammad (PBUH) provide valuable lessons for modern leaders. In today's fast-paced world, where communication is often rushed and superficial, the art of listening is more important than ever. Here are some ways that modern leaders can apply active listening to build stronger connections and lead more effectively:

Prioritise Listening in Meetings and Conversations

In leadership, it's easy to fall into the trap of focusing on what you want to say rather than what others are saying. To be an effective leader, it's important to prioritise listening in meetings and conversations. This means giving others the space to share their thoughts and concerns and making a conscious effort to understand their perspectives.

By prioritising listening, leaders can make more informed decisions, foster a collaborative environment, and build stronger relationships with their team members.

Encourage Open Dialogue

Effective leaders create an environment where open dialogue is encouraged and valued. This involves fostering a culture of transparency, where team members feel comfortable sharing their ideas, concerns, and feedback without fear of judgment or retaliation.

Encouraging open dialogue requires leaders to listen actively and respond with empathy and respect. By doing so, they can tap into their team's collective wisdom and make more inclusive and well-rounded decisions.

Practice Empathy in Decision-Making

Empathy is a key component of active listening and is essential for effective decision-making. Leaders should strive to understand the emotions and perspectives of those affected by their decisions and consider these factors when making choices.

Practising empathy in decision-making not only leads to more compassionate and fair outcomes but also strengthens the trust and loyalty of team members and stakeholders.

Provide Constructive Feedback

Active listening is not just about understanding others; it's also about providing thoughtful and constructive feedback. When giving feedback, leaders should listen carefully to the other person's perspective and frame their feedback in a way that is supportive and solution-oriented.

By providing feedback based on active listening, leaders can help others grow and develop while maintaining positive and respectful relationships.

Lead by Example

Leaders set the tone for the entire organisation, and their behaviour serves as a model for others to follow. By consistently practising active listening, leaders can set a powerful example for their team and create a culture where listening is valued and prioritised.

Leading by example in active listening not only strengthens the leader's own relationships but also encourages others to adopt the same approach in their interactions.

Chapter Six

Decision-Making and Problem-Solving

The Prophet's approach to decision-making was both inclusive and deeply consultative. Embracing the principle of shura, or seeking counsel, he made sure everyone had a voice. It was about building a sense of ownership and unity. Imagine the impact today, where a similar approach could build team spirit and lead to decisions enriched by diverse perspectives.

Wisdom, or hikmah, and foresight were hallmarks of the Prophet's problem-solving skills. He had an uncanny ability to see potential challenges and come up with thoughtful solutions. In our fast-paced world, this kind of proactive thinking is invaluable. It's about being prepared, anticipating issues, and addressing them before they turn into bigger problems.

The Prophet's approach to resolving conflicts was marked by fairness and justice. He listened to all sides with impartiality, ensuring everyone felt heard and respected. This not only resolved disputes effectively but also built a foundation of trust and integrity within the community. Today's leaders can learn a lot from this approach—applying these principles can help find fair solutions that uphold ethical standards.

Consider how these methods can transform leadership today. By seeking advice, using wisdom and foresight, and handling conflicts with fairness, leaders can guide their teams through the complexities of modern business. It's about blending timeless wisdom with current challenges, making decisions that are effective and grounded in integrity and collective strength.

Prophetic Approaches to Decision-Making

Seeking counsel (shura) and consultation in business decisions

Prophet Muhammad (PBUH) frequently employed shura, valuing the input and advice of his companions in various matters. This consultative approach not only led to more informed and robust decisions but also fostered a sense of unity and collective responsibility. By integrating shura into modern business practices, leaders can enhance their decision-making processes and build stronger, more cohesive teams.

The Principle of Shura

Shura is deeply rooted in Islamic teachings and is emphasised in the Quran. The principle involves seeking advice and consultation from others, particularly those who have relevant knowledge or experience. This practice is not only a demonstration of humility but also a recognition that collective wisdom often surpasses individual insight.

> *"And those who have responded to their lord and established prayer and whose affair is [determined by] consultation among themselves, and from what We have provided them, they spend." (Quran 42:38)*

This verse highlights the importance of consultation in the decision-making process, underscoring that it is a collective affair involving input from various stakeholders.

Leaders who practice shura recognise that wisdom is not confined to the top ranks but can be found throughout the organisation. This approach builds a culture of mutual respect and continuous learning.

The Prophet's use of shura illustrates that true leadership involves listening as much as speaking. His willingness to seek advice, even from those who might have seemed less experienced, showed profound humility and respect. This practice created an environment where everyone felt empowered to contribute, knowing their insights were valued.

In a modern business context, integrating shura means creating spaces where open dialogue is encouraged. This can be through regular team meetings, brainstorming sessions, or anonymous feedback systems. The goal is to ensure that all voices are heard and diverse perspectives are considered.

The inclusive nature of shura also means being open to ideas that challenge the status quo. Leaders must be willing to adapt and change course based on sound advice. This flexibility can lead to more innovative solutions and a more agile organisation capable of navigating complex challenges.

Prophetic Examples of Shura

Prophet Muhammad (PBUH) consistently sought the counsel of his companions, even in critical situations. This approach not only ensured that decisions were well-informed but also strengthened the bonds of trust and respect within the community.

One notable example of shura is the Battle of Badr. As the Muslim army approached the battlefield, Prophet Muhammad (PBUH) consulted his companions about the best location to encamp. One companion,

Al-Hubab ibn al-Mundhir, suggested a different location that offered strategic advantages. The Prophet accepted this advice, which significantly contributed to the Muslims' victory.

> *"The Prophet said to his companions, 'Advise me, O people.' Al-Hubab ibn al-Mundhir said, 'This is not a suitable place, O Messenger of Allah. Let us go to the well nearest to the enemy.' The Prophet accepted his suggestion." (Sahih Bukhari)*

This example demonstrates the Prophet's openness to advice and his willingness to change plans based on sound counsel.

Benefits of Shura in Business Decisions

Implementing shura in business decisions offers numerous benefits. It ensures that decisions are well-rounded, reduces the risk of errors, and enhances team cohesion. Here are some key advantages:

Diverse Perspectives: Consultation brings together diverse perspectives, enriching the decision-making process. Different team members may offer unique insights based on their experiences and expertise, leading to more comprehensive and innovative solutions.

Increased Buy-In: When team members are involved in the decision-making process, they are more likely to feel a sense of ownership and commitment to the outcomes. This buy-in is crucial for successful implementation and collective effort.

Improved Morale: Seeking counsel demonstrates respect and appreciation for team members' contributions. This practice can significantly boost morale, fostering a positive and inclusive work environment.

Enhanced Problem-Solving: Consultation encourages critical thinking and collaborative problem-solving. By considering multiple viewpoints, potential issues can be identified and addressed proactively, leading to more effective and sustainable solutions.

Implementing Shura in Modern Business

Integrating shura into modern business practices requires a structured approach to ensure that consultation is effective and productive. Here are some practical steps for implementing shura in business decisions:

Identify Key Stakeholders: Identify the individuals or groups who have relevant knowledge or are affected by the decision. These stakeholders should be included in the consultation process to ensure that all perspectives are considered.

Create an Open Environment: Foster an environment where team members feel comfortable sharing their thoughts and ideas. This can be achieved through regular meetings, open-door policies, and encouraging open dialogue.

Establish Clear Objectives: Clearly define the objectives of the consultation process. This ensures that discussions remain focused and aligned with the overall goals of the decision-making process.

Encourage Active Participation: Encourage all participants to actively engage in the consultation process. This can be facilitated by asking open-ended questions, seeking feedback, and ensuring that everyone has an opportunity to contribute.

Evaluate and Synthesise Input: Evaluate the input received from the consultation process, identifying common themes and key insights. Synthesise this information to inform the final decision, ensuring that it reflects the collective wisdom of the team.

Communicate Decisions Transparently: Once a decision has been made, communicate it clearly and transparently to all stakeholders. Explain how the consultation process influenced the decision and highlight the contributions of team members.

Follow Up and Reflect: After the decision has been implemented, follow up with the team to assess its impact. Reflect on the consultation process and identify any areas for improvement, ensuring that future consultations are even more effective.

Case Study: Implementing Shura in a Modern Company

Consider a mid-sized tech company facing a strategic decision about launching a new product. The CEO decides to implement shura to ensure a well-rounded decision. Here's how the process unfolds:

Identify Key Stakeholders: The CEO includes senior managers, product developers, marketing staff, and customer service representatives in the consultation process.

Create an Open Environment: A series of meetings and brainstorming sessions are organised, where team members are encouraged to share their insights and concerns openly.

Establish Clear Objectives: The objective is to gather diverse perspectives on the product's potential market fit, customer needs, and possible challenges.

Encourage Active Participation: Team members are asked to provide detailed feedback and suggestions. The CEO ensures that everyone has a chance to speak and that all ideas are considered.

Evaluate and Synthesise Input: The input is reviewed, and key themes such as market demand, competitive landscape, and product features are identified. A decision is made to proceed with the product launch, incorporating several suggestions from the consultation.

Communicate Decisions Transparently: The CEO communicates the final decision to the entire company, explaining how the input influenced the decision and acknowledging the contributions of team members.

Follow Up and Reflect: After the product launch, the team regularly reviews its progress and discusses any adjustments needed. The CEO reflects on the consultation process and notes areas for improvement for future decisions.

Applying wisdom (hikmah) and foresight in problem-solving

Wisdom encompasses deep understanding, sound judgment, and the ability to see the broader picture. Coupled with foresight, it allows leaders to navigate complexities and make decisions that ensure long-term success and stability. Prophet Muhammad (PBUH) exemplified the application of wisdom and foresight in problem-solving, offering timeless lessons for modern leaders.

The Concept of Hikmah

Hikmah, or wisdom, is highly valued in Islam. It is the ability to make sound decisions based on knowledge, experience, and a deep understanding of the situation. The Quran frequently emphasises the importance of wisdom:

> *"He grants wisdom to whom He pleases; and he to whom wisdom is granted receives indeed a benefit overflowing; but none will grasp the Message but men of understanding." (Quran 2:269)*

This verse highlights that wisdom is a divine gift, and those who possess it are truly fortunate. Wisdom enables leaders to approach problems thoughtfully and make decisions that are not only effective but also just and beneficial.

Prophetic Examples of Hikmah

Prophet Muhammad (PBUH) demonstrated exceptional wisdom and leadership in various aspects of his life. His approach to problem-solving was marked by deep understanding, patience, and strategic thinking.

Handling the Hypocrites

One notable example of the Prophet's wisdom is how he dealt with the hypocrites in Medina. Rather than confronting them aggressively and causing internal strife, he chose a more nuanced approach. The Prophet (PBUH) understood the delicate social fabric of the community and acted in a way that maintained harmony while addressing the underlying issues. This method preserved the unity and stability of the Muslim community.

Reconciliation with Abu Sufyan

The reconciliation with Abu Sufyan, a former adversary, showcases the Prophet's profound wisdom in fostering peace and unity. By treating Abu Sufyan with respect and offering forgiveness after the conquest of Mecca, the Prophet (PBUH) turned a potential enemy into a staunch supporter of Islam. This strategic move helped to solidify the newly unified Muslim community.

Prophetic Examples of Foresight

Prophet Muhammad (PBUH) demonstrated remarkable foresight in his leadership. His ability to anticipate future events and plan accordingly ensured the growth and stability of the Muslim community.

The Migration to Abyssinia

The migration (Hijra) to Abyssinia was a strategic move demonstrating the Prophet's foresight. Facing severe persecution in Mecca, Prophet Muhammad (PBUH) advised a group of his followers to seek refuge in Abyssinia, where they were received warmly by the Christian king, Negus. This move not only protected the early Muslims but also established an early example of interfaith harmony and diplomacy.

> *"If you were to go to Abyssinia, you would find a king there who does not wrong anyone. It is a land of truthfulness." (Sahih Bukhari)*

Establishing the Constitution of Medina

Upon arriving in Medina, the Prophet (PBUH) demonstrated his foresight by establishing the Constitution of Medina. This charter outlined the rights and responsibilities of all inhabitants, including Muslims, Jews, and other tribes. It promoted social cohesion, justice, and mutual respect, ensuring a stable and unified community.

The Alliance with the Bedouins

The strategic alliances formed with various Bedouin tribes also highlight the Prophet's foresight. By securing these alliances, the Prophet (PBUH) ensured the safety and supply lines for the Muslim community, effectively surrounding Mecca and reducing the threat from hostile tribes.

Applying Wisdom in Modern Problem-Solving

Modern leaders can draw on the concept of hikmah to enhance their problem-solving abilities. Here are some ways to apply wisdom in contemporary settings:

Deep Understanding: Wisdom begins with a deep understanding of the problem. Leaders should gather comprehensive information, consider various perspectives, and analyse the root causes of the issue. This thorough understanding lays the foundation for sound decision-making.

Sound Judgment: Using sound judgment involves weighing the pros and cons of different solutions and considering their long-term implications. Leaders should avoid hasty decisions and take the time to reflect on the best course of action.

Patience and Restraint: Patience is a key component of wisdom. Leaders should exercise restraint and avoid reactive decisions. Taking the time to think through problems carefully can lead to more effective and sustainable solutions.

Ethical Considerations: Wisdom also involves making decisions that are ethical and just. Leaders should consider the broader impact of their decisions on stakeholders and strive to uphold integrity and fairness.

The Role of Foresight

Foresight is the ability to anticipate future challenges and opportunities. It complements wisdom by allowing leaders to prepare for what lies ahead and mitigate potential risks.

Strategic Planning: Strategic planning is a practical application of foresight. Leaders should set long-term goals, anticipate future trends, and develop plans that position their organisations for success. This involves not only responding to current challenges but also preparing for future changes.

Risk Management: Effective risk management requires foresight. Leaders should identify potential risks, assess their impact, and develop strategies to mitigate them. This proactive approach helps organisations navigate uncertainties and avoid crises.

Innovation and Adaptability: Foresight also involves being open to innovation and adaptability. Leaders should stay informed about industry trends, technological advancements, and changing market conditions. This awareness allows them to adapt quickly and seize new opportunities.

Resolving Conflicts and Challenges

In any organisation, conflicts and disputes are inevitable. These conflicts arise from differing perspectives, competing interests, and the dynamic nature of human interactions. Effective leaders must possess the skills to address these conflicts with fairness and justice, ensuring that resolutions are not only equitable but also promote long-term harmony and trust.

The life of Prophet Muhammad (PBUH) offers valuable insights into resolving conflicts justly and fairly. His approaches provide timeless lessons for contemporary leaders on maintaining integrity and fostering a cohesive environment.

Fairness and justice are fundamental principles in conflict resolution. When leaders resolve disputes with these values at the forefront, they maintain trust and credibility within their organisations. Ensuring that all parties involved in a conflict are heard, that their concerns are addressed, and that the outcomes are equitable is crucial for fostering a culture of respect and cooperation.

The Quran emphasises the importance of justice in all affairs, highlighting that impartiality and integrity are essential, even when these principles challenge personal biases or relationships.

Quranic Guidance on Justice

The Quran serves as a guide for all aspects of life, including conflict resolution. It stresses the necessity of standing firm in justice, as reflected in the verse:

> "O you who have believed, be persistently standing firm in justice, witnesses for Allah, even if it be against yourselves or parents and relatives." (Quran 4:135)

This verse underscores the importance of maintaining justice without letting personal relationships or biases interfere. It reminds leaders that justice must be upheld at all times, even when it is difficult or involves self-reflection and accountability.

Prophetic Examples of Fairness and Justice

Prophet Muhammad (PBUH) exemplified fairness and justice in his approach to resolving conflicts. His methods were characterised by impartiality, empathy, and a deep commitment to ethical principles. These qualities are evident in several notable incidents from his life, which offer profound lessons for modern leaders.

The Case of the Stolen Shield

One significant example is the case of the stolen shield involving Safwan ibn Umayyah. In this incident, a Muslim man was wrongfully accused of theft. The matter was brought before the Prophet, who conducted a thorough investigation to uncover the truth.

It was eventually revealed that the real culprit was not the accused Muslim but someone else entirely. The Prophet ensured that justice was served by holding the true thief accountable, demonstrating his commitment to fairness regardless of the individuals involved.

This incident also highlights the importance of evidence in adjudicating disputes. The Prophet's approach emphasises that justice must be based on facts and fairness, rather than assumptions or biases.

> *"The proof is on the claimant, and the oath is on the one who denies." (Sahih Bukhari)*

This principle serves as a foundational guideline for resolving conflicts, ensuring that decisions are made based on solid evidence.

The Incident of Fatimah Bint Qays

Another profound example of the Prophet's commitment to justice was his handling of a case involving theft by a woman from the noble Makhzum tribe, named Fatimah bint Qays. The community hesitated to impose the prescribed punishment due to her noble lineage. Addressing this, the Prophet famously stated:

> *"By Allah, if Fatimah, the daughter of Muhammad, were to steal, I would have her hand cut off." (Sahih Bukhari)*

This declaration underscored the principle that justice applies equally to everyone, regardless of their social status or relationship to the Prophet. It was a powerful statement against nepotism and partiality, reinforcing that no one is above the law. The Prophet's firm stance on this issue ensured that justice was upheld, even when it involved difficult decisions and the potential for social backlash.

Resolving Tribal Conflicts with Justice

The Prophet's wisdom and fairness were also evident in his handling of tribal conflicts. One notable example is his mediation between the tribes of Aws and Khazraj in Medina, who had a history of longstanding feuds. When disputes arose between these tribes, the Prophet acted as a mediator, approaching the situation with fairness and seeking equitable solutions that respected the rights and interests of all parties involved.

The Prophet's approach emphasised mutual respect and understanding, which ultimately led to lasting peace between the previously warring factions. His ability to resolve these tribal conflicts with justice not only strengthened the bonds within the Muslim community but also set a precedent for future generations on the importance of fairness in conflict resolution.

Principles of Fair and Just Conflict Resolution

To effectively resolve conflicts, leaders must adhere to several key principles that ensure fairness and justice are upheld throughout the process.

These principles include impartiality, transparency, empathy, consistency, and adherence to ethical considerations.

Impartiality

Impartiality is critical in conflict resolution. Leaders must approach disputes without bias, ensuring all parties are treated equally. This involves listening to all sides of the story and making decisions based on facts and evidence rather than personal preferences or relationships. The Prophet Muhammad's handling of the stolen shield case exemplifies this principle, as he conducted a thorough investigation to ensure that justice was served, regardless of the individuals involved.

Transparency

Transparency in the decision-making process builds trust and credibility. Leaders should clearly communicate the steps they are taking to resolve the conflict, the criteria for their decisions, and the rationale behind the final outcome. This openness helps all parties understand that the process is fair and objective, and it reduces the potential for misunderstandings or feelings of resentment.

Empathy

Empathy involves understanding and acknowledging the feelings and perspectives of all parties involved. Leaders should demonstrate genuine concern for the well-being of those in conflict, which can help de-escalate tensions and foster a cooperative atmosphere. The Prophet's approach to resolving conflicts was always marked by empathy, as he sought to address not only the factual aspects of the dispute but also the emotional needs of the parties involved.

Consistency

Applying rules and policies consistently is essential for maintaining fairness in conflict resolution. Leaders should ensure that similar conflicts are resolved in similar ways, avoiding arbitrary or preferential treatment. This consistency reinforces the credibility of the leadership and ensures that all members of the organisation feel that they are treated equitably.

Ethical Considerations

Ethical considerations should guide all aspects of conflict resolution. Leaders must uphold principles of honesty, integrity, and justice, ensuring that their actions align with the organisation's core values. The Prophet Muhammad's unwavering commitment to justice, even when it involved difficult decisions or personal relationships, serves as a powerful example of the importance of ethics in leadership.

Steps for Addressing Conflicts with Fairness and Justice

Resolving conflicts effectively requires a structured approach that ensures all aspects of the dispute are addressed fairly and justly. The following steps outline a process leaders can follow to achieve equitable outcomes.

Identify the Root Cause

Understanding the root cause of the conflict is the first step in resolving it effectively. This involves gathering information from all parties involved and identifying the underlying issues that have led to the dispute. By focusing on the root cause, leaders can address the core problems rather than just treating the symptoms.

Facilitate Open Dialogue

Creating a safe space for open dialogue allows parties to express their concerns and perspectives. Leaders should facilitate these discussions, ensuring that everyone has an opportunity to speak and be heard. This process helps to uncover hidden issues and provides a platform for all parties to share their views, which is essential for finding a fair resolution.

Evaluate Evidence

Decisions should be based on facts and evidence. Leaders must evaluate the information objectively, avoiding assumptions or biases. The Prophet's approach in the case of the stolen shield, where he conducted a thorough investigation to uncover the truth, exemplifies the importance of evidence-based decision-making in conflict resolution.

Develop Fair Solutions

Solutions should address the needs and concerns of all parties involved. Leaders should aim for win-win outcomes that promote long-term harmony and cooperation. This approach not only resolves the immediate conflict but also strengthens relationships and builds trust within the organisation.

Communicate the Decision

Clearly communicating the decision and the reasoning behind it is crucial for maintaining transparency and trust. This transparency helps build confidence in the fairness of the process and ensures that all parties understand the basis for the resolution.

Follow Up

Following up after the resolution helps ensure that the conflict has been effectively addressed and that the parties are satisfied with the outcome. It also provides an opportunity to address any lingering issues or concerns, reinforcing the leader's commitment to fairness and justice.

Finding Win-Win Solutions Based on Islamic Principles

A win-win solution is one where all parties feel their needs and interests have been addressed. Unlike zero-sum outcomes, where one party's gain is another's loss, win-win solutions seek mutual benefit. This approach resolves the immediate conflict, strengthens relationships, and builds trust.

Islamic teachings offer valuable guidance for finding win-win solutions. Core principles such as justice (adl), empathy (rahma), and mutual consultation (shura) provide a foundation for resolving conflicts in a way that benefits all parties.

Justice is a cornerstone of Islamic ethics. The Quran repeatedly emphasises the importance of fairness and equity in all dealings. In the context of conflict resolution, ensuring justice means considering the rights and interests of all parties and striving for outcomes that are fair and equitable.

Empathy involves understanding and sharing the feelings of others. Prophet Muhammad (PBUH) exemplified empathy in his interactions, always considering the well-being of others. In conflict resolution, empathy means actively listening to the concerns of all parties and addressing their emotional and practical needs.

Shura, or mutual consultation, is a vital principle in Islamic decision-making. It involves seeking the advice and input of others to reach well-rounded decisions. Incorporating shura in conflict resolution ensures that diverse perspectives are considered, leading to more balanced and acceptable solutions. This collaborative approach enhances the quality of decisions and builds stronger relationships.

The Role of Perspective in Conflict Resolution

Another crucial aspect of resolving conflicts and finding win-win solutions is understanding that not all apparent losses are true losses, and not all apparent gains are true gains. The Quran addresses this concept, reminding us to approach conflicts with an open mind and to recognise that outcomes may have hidden benefits or drawbacks that are not immediately apparent.

> *"... But perhaps you hate a thing and it is good for you; and perhaps you love a thing and it is bad for you. And Allah Knows, while you know not." (Quran 2:216)*

This verse encourages leaders to maintain perspective when resolving conflicts, acknowledging that what may seem unfavourable at first could lead to positive outcomes in the long term. By keeping this perspective in mind, leaders can make more thoughtful and balanced decisions, ultimately leading to more effective conflict resolution.

Stress Management in Decision-Making

Decision-making is an essential part of leadership, and when the stakes are high, it often comes with significant stress. The ability to manage this stress effectively is crucial for making sound, rational decisions.

Stress in decision-making can arise from various sources, such as the urgency of the situation, the potential consequences of the decision, or the complexity of the factors involved. When stress is not managed properly, it can cloud judgment, narrow focus, and lead to decisions driven more by emotion than by reason.

Prophet Muhammad (PBUH) exemplified how to handle stress in decision-making with grace, patience, and wisdom. His life is filled with instances where he faced immense pressure, yet his decisions were marked by clarity, foresight, and a deep sense of responsibility. These examples provide timeless lessons for leaders and individuals facing difficult decisions.

The Battle of the Trench

One of the most notable examples of the Prophet's stress management in decision-making occurred during the Battle of the Trench. The Muslim community in Medina faced a dire threat as the Quraysh and their allies formed a massive coalition to attack the city. The situation was critical, and the pressure on the Prophet was immense. In response to this overwhelming threat, the Prophet consulted with his companions, including Salman al-Farsi, who suggested an innovative defensive strategy—digging a trench around Medina. This tactic was unfamiliar to the Arabs, but the Prophet recognised its potential effectiveness.

Despite the looming danger, the Prophet remained calm and focused, leading by example. He personally participated in the laborious task of digging the trench, working alongside his companions. His involvement and leadership during this stressful time were crucial in maintaining the morale and unity of the Muslim community. The trench successfully thwarted the enemy's advance, demonstrating how the Prophet's ability to manage stress led to a strategic and successful decision.

The Incident of the Hypocrites

Another instance of the Prophet's stress management in decision-making can be seen in his handling of the hypocrites (Munafiqeen) within the Muslim community. The leader of the hypocrites, Abdullah ibn Ubayy, caused significant harm through his deceitful actions, spreading discord and attempting to undermine the Prophet's leadership. This situation was incredibly stressful, as the Prophet had to deal with internal betrayal while maintaining the unity of the Muslim community.

Despite the danger posed by the hypocrites, the Prophet chose not to publicly confront them or punish them harshly. Instead, he exercised patience and wisdom, understanding that a direct confrontation could lead to greater division and unrest within the community. The Prophet's decision to tolerate the hypocrites' behaviour, while continuing to guide the community with compassion and integrity, exemplifies his ability to manage stress and prioritise the well-being of the entire Muslim ummah.

This approach allowed the Prophet to maintain the cohesion of the Muslim community, avoiding unnecessary conflicts and focusing on more pressing external threats. The incident highlights the importance of strategic patience and the ability to see the bigger picture when making decisions under stress.

The Decision at the Battle of Hunayn

The Battle of Hunayn presents another example of the Prophet's stress management in decision-making. After the conquest of Mecca, the Prophet and his followers faced a new challenge from the tribes of Hawazin and Thaqif, who assembled a large army to resist the Muslim expansion. The battle was intense, and at one point, the Muslim forces faced a significant setback as they were ambushed and temporarily thrown into disarray.

In this moment of crisis, the Prophet remained calm and composed. He rallied his troops, encouraging them to stay firm and trust in Allah. His leadership during this stressful situation was crucial in turning the tide of the battle. The Prophet's ability to manage stress and inspire confidence in his followers helped the Muslims regroup and ultimately secure a decisive victory.

The decision to stand firm in the face of adversity, rather than retreating or panicking, demonstrates the Prophet's unwavering faith and his ability to lead effectively under pressure. This incident underscores the importance of maintaining composure and relying on inner strength during moments of intense stress.

The Confrontation with the Tribe of Banu Qurayza

Following the Battle of the Trench, the Prophet faced a difficult and stressful decision regarding the fate of the Jewish tribe of Banu Qurayza, who had betrayed the Muslims by allying with the Quraysh during the siege of Medina. The betrayal by Banu Qurayza was a severe breach of their agreement with the Muslims, and the situation required a decision that would uphold justice while also considering the long-term implications for the community.

The Prophet delegated the decision to Sa'd ibn Mu'adh, a respected leader from the Aws tribe, who was known for his wisdom and fairness. Sa'd's decision was to execute the men of Banu Qurayza and enslave the women and children, which was a harsh but common practice in that era for treason. The Prophet accepted this decision, understanding that it was necessary to maintain the security and stability of the Muslim community.

This incident highlights the Prophet's ability to manage the stress of making a deeply consequential decision by seeking the counsel of a trusted companion and ensuring that the decision was grounded in justice. While the outcome was severe, it was seen as necessary to protect the Muslim community from future betrayals and to establish a precedent for the treatment of those who violated their agreements.

The Prophet's Response to the Death of His Son, Ibrahim

The death of the Prophet's young son, Ibrahim, was a deeply personal and stressful event. The Prophet's love for his son was profound, and his grief was immense. Yet, even in this moment of intense personal sorrow, the Prophet demonstrated remarkable composure and strength.

When Ibrahim passed away, the Prophet held him in his arms and wept, saying,

> *"The eyes shed tears and the heart is grieved, but we do not say anything except that which pleases our Lord. O Ibrahim! Indeed, we are grieved by your separation"*
> *(Sahih Bukhari)*

Despite the overwhelming grief, the Prophet's words reflected his deep faith and acceptance of Allah's will. He managed his stress and sorrow through prayer, patience, and reliance on Allah, setting an example for his followers on how to handle personal loss with dignity and grace.

This incident illustrates how the Prophet managed stress through a combination of emotional expression, spiritual reflection, and a deep connection with Allah. His response to the death of his son provides a powerful lesson in how to navigate the emotional stress of personal tragedy while maintaining faith and composure.

The Prophet's Decision During the Year of Sorrow

The Year of Sorrow (Aam al-Huzn) was a particularly difficult period in the life of Prophet Muhammad (PBUH), marked by the deaths of his beloved wife Khadijah and his uncle Abu Talib, who had been his protector and supporter. These losses were deeply personal and had significant implications for the Prophet's mission, as they left him vulnerable to increased hostility and persecution from the Quraysh.

During this time of immense personal grief and stress, the Prophet made the difficult decision to travel to Ta'if, seeking support from the local leaders. Unfortunately, this decision led to one of the most painful experiences in the Prophet's life, as he was rejected and mistreated by the people of Ta'if. Despite this additional hardship, the Prophet's response was one of remarkable patience and reliance on Allah.

After being driven out of Ta'if and subjected to physical abuse, the Prophet sought refuge in a garden, where he prayed to Allah for strength and guidance. His prayer, known as the "Dua of Ta'if," is a profound expression of his faith and his ability to manage stress through spiritual connection. In his prayer, the Prophet expressed his vulnerability and his trust in Allah's mercy, saying, "If You are not angry with me, I do not care what happens to me."

The Prophet's decision to seek help from Ta'if, despite the outcome, reflects his relentless dedication to his mission and his ability to manage stress through unwavering faith. His resilience in the face of such personal and professional setbacks provides a powerful lesson in how to persevere through difficult times by maintaining a strong connection with one's faith.

The Handling of the Rumours After the Battle of Uhud

After the Battle of Uhud, rumours spread that the Prophet had been killed in the battle. This caused widespread panic and despair among the Muslims, who were already demoralised by their defeat. The Prophet's first priority was to manage the stress and fear that had gripped his followers.

Despite being wounded, the Prophet quickly took control of the situation. He rallied his companions, dispelled the rumours of his death, and organised a retreat to a more defensible position. His ability to stay calm and decisive in the face of such stress was crucial in preventing further chaos and maintaining the cohesion of the Muslim army.

The Prophet's management of this situation highlights his capacity to think clearly and act effectively under pressure. By quickly addressing the rumour's and leading his followers with confidence, he was able to stabilize the situation and prevent the defeat from turning into a total disaster. This incident underscores the importance of clear communication and decisive action in managing stress during critical moments.

The Decision to Emigrate to Medina

The decision to emigrate from Mecca to Medina, known as the Hijrah, was one of the most significant and stressful decisions in the life of the Prophet Muhammad (PBUH). The persecution of Muslims in Mecca had reached unbearable levels, and the situation had become increasingly dangerous. The Prophet had to make the difficult decision to leave his birthplace, a city that held immense personal and spiritual significance, to ensure the safety and future of the Muslim community.

The decision to migrate was fraught with risks. The journey to Medina was long and perilous, and there was the constant threat of being pursued and attacked by the Quraysh. Despite these challenges, the Prophet managed the stress of the situation with remarkable calm and foresight. He meticulously planned the migration, coordinating with the Muslims in Medina to ensure a safe and orderly transition.

The Prophet's decision to migrate was not only a strategic move but also a deeply spiritual one. He placed his trust in Allah, knowing that the Hijrah was a divinely ordained step in the establishment of the Muslim ummah. The success of the migration, and the subsequent establishment of the first Islamic state in Medina, is a testament to the Prophet's ability to manage stress through careful planning, trust in divine guidance, and unwavering commitment to his mission.

The Prophet's Response to the False Accusation Against Maria al-Qibtiyya

Another significant example of the Prophet's stress management in decision-making is his response to the false accusation against Maria al-Qibtiyya, one of his wives. The rumour that she had committed adultery with a man named Ma'ish was a serious accusation that could have led to severe consequences, both personally and within the Muslim community.

The Prophet, once again, did not rush to judgment. Instead, he conducted a thorough investigation, showing his commitment to justice and truth even under the stress of personal scandal. The investigation revealed that the accusation was baseless, and Maria's innocence was confirmed.

The Prophet's handling of this situation demonstrates his ability to manage the stress of personal and public pressure while ensuring that justice was served. His decision to approach the matter with caution and fairness, rather than reacting impulsively, underscores the importance of maintaining composure and integrity in decision-making.

Stress is an inevitable part of decision-making, especially for leaders who bear the responsibility of guiding others and making choices that can have profound consequences. The ability to manage this stress effectively is what distinguishes great leaders from the rest. The life of Prophet Muhammad (PBUH) offers numerous examples of how to handle stress in decision-making, providing valuable lessons that are still relevant today.

Chapter Seven

Leading by Example

True leaders don't just talk about ethical behaviour—they live it. By consistently making decisions that reflect their values, they show their teams that ethics are non-negotiable, fostering a culture where doing the right thing becomes second nature.

Practising humility, patience, and resilience in leadership further strengthens this ethical foundation. Humility allows leaders to acknowledge their limitations and seek input from others, fostering collaboration and continuous learning. Patience helps them navigate challenges without succumbing to frustration or haste, ensuring thoughtful and balanced decisions.

Resilience, meanwhile, empowers leaders to stay steadfast in the face of adversity, inspiring their teams to persevere through difficulties. These qualities, demonstrated consistently, make leaders approachable and trustworthy, reinforcing their role as ethical exemplars.

When leaders show their unwavering dedication through hard work and perseverance, they motivate their teams to adopt the same level of commitment. This kind of leadership builds a strong sense of purpose and alignment, driving everyone towards common objectives with renewed vigour.

Drawing inspiration from the life of Prophet Muhammad (PBUH), we see how his actions consistently reflected his teachings. He led by example, whether it was through his honesty in trade, his compassion in community interactions, or his resilience in the face of persecution. His leadership was marked by a deep sense of responsibility and care for his followers, setting a timeless example of ethical and inspirational leadership.

Role Modelling Ethical Leadership Behaviours

Setting a positive example for employees and stakeholders

Ethical leadership is crucial for several reasons. It builds trust, fosters a positive work environment, and enhances the reputation of the organisation. Employees look to their leaders for cues on how to behave, and when leaders consistently demonstrate ethical behaviour, it encourages employees to follow suit.

This alignment between leadership and employee behaviour is essential for creating a cohesive and principled organisational culture.

The Story of the Prophet's Business Dealings

Before his prophethood, Muhammad (PBUH) was a successful merchant known for his honesty and integrity. His reputation as Al-Amin, the trustworthy, was built on years of transparent and fair business practices. He never engaged in deceitful tactics or took advantage of others, even when it could have been profitable.

This unwavering commitment to honesty set a powerful example for his contemporaries and established a foundation of trust. For modern leaders, this illustrates the importance of maintaining integrity in all dealings. Transparent communication and honest practices build trust and foster a loyal and motivated workforce.

Upon arriving in Medina, the Prophet (PBUH) participated in the construction of the mosque alongside his companions. This act of humility and shared labour fostered a strong sense of community and mutual respect.

Modern leaders who work alongside their teams build solidarity and respect. This approach promotes a culture of collaboration and shows that no task is beneath the leader.

Setting a Positive Example

Role modelling ethical behaviour means that leaders must consistently demonstrate the values and principles they expect from others. This consistency is key to fostering an ethical culture. Here are some ways leaders can set a positive example for their employees and stakeholders:

Demonstrating Integrity

Integrity is about being honest and having strong moral principles. Leaders with integrity do what they say and say what they do. They are transparent in their actions and decisions, ensuring that there is no discrepancy between their words and deeds.

Example: A leader who admits to a mistake rather than covering it up demonstrates integrity. This action not only corrects the mistake but also builds trust and shows that honesty is valued over protecting one's image.

Making Fair Decisions

Ethical leaders ensure that their decisions are fair and just. They consider the impact of their choices on all stakeholders and strive to act in ways that are equitable.

Example: When faced with budget cuts, a fair leader might choose to implement salary reductions across all levels of the organisation rather than laying off a significant portion of the workforce. This approach spreads the burden more evenly and demonstrates a commitment to fairness.

Treating Others with Respect

Respect is fundamental to ethical leadership. Leaders should treat all employees, regardless of their position, with dignity and respect. This means listening to their concerns, valuing their contributions, and treating them as partners in the organisation's success.

Example: A leader who makes time for regular one-on-one meetings with team members, listens to their feedback, and implements their suggestions shows respect and values their input.

Leading by Example

Leaders must embody the behaviours they want to see in their employees. This means adhering to the same standards and expectations they set for others.

Example: If punctuality is important, a leader should consistently be on time for meetings. If collaboration is valued, a leader should actively participate in team projects and show a willingness to collaborate.

Communicating Ethical Standards

Clear communication of ethical standards and expectations is crucial. Leaders should regularly discuss the organisation's values and ethical guidelines, ensuring that all employees understand and are committed to upholding them.

Example: Regular training sessions on ethical conduct, combined with open forums for discussing ethical dilemmas, can help reinforce the importance of ethics in the workplace.

Benefits of Role Modelling Ethical Leadership

When leaders consistently model ethical behaviour, the benefits are manifold. It leads to increased employee engagement, improved morale, and a stronger sense of community within the organisation.

Employees are more likely to take pride in their work and the organisation they represent. This commitment translates into better performance, higher productivity, and greater innovation.

Enhanced Employee Engagement: Employees who see their leaders behaving ethically are more likely to be engaged and committed to their work. They feel valued and respected, which boosts their motivation and performance.

Improved Morale: A workplace that values ethics is a positive and supportive environment. This leads to higher morale, as employees feel good about their work and their contributions to the organisation's success.

Stronger Community and Culture: Ethical leadership fosters a sense of community within the organisation. Employees feel connected to each other and to the organisation's mission and values. This sense of belonging enhances collaboration and teamwork.

Practising humility, patience, and resilience in leadership

Humility in leadership involves recognising one's limitations, valuing the contributions of others, and leading with a sense of service rather than authority. Humility is not a sign of weakness but rather a demonstration of self-awareness and respect for others.

Prophetic Example of Humility

Prophet Muhammad (PBUH) embodied humility in every aspect of his life. Despite his immense status and responsibilities, he lived modestly and engaged in everyday tasks alongside his followers. His humility was not an act but a genuine expression of his character.

Helping with Household Chores

Aisha (may Allah be pleased with her) narrated that the Prophet would mend his own clothes, repair his shoes, and assist with household chores. This was a profound demonstration of humility, as he did not see any task as beneath him, despite being the leader of the Muslim community.

Interacting with All Social Classes

The Prophet treated people of all backgrounds with kindness and respect. Whether interacting with the wealthy or the poor, he maintained the same level of respect and compassion. This is highlighted in his interactions with the slaves and the marginalised members of society, whom he treated with dignity and empathy.

Riding a Mule

During the conquest of Mecca, Prophet Muhammad (PBUH) entered the city riding a mule, with his head bowed in humility. He did not enter as a conqueror seeking revenge, but as a humble servant of Allah, showing mercy and forgiveness to those who had previously persecuted him and his followers.

> *"The most beloved of people to Allah are those who are most beneficial to people." (Al-Mu'jam Al-Awsat)*

This saying underscores the Prophet's focus on serving others, a key aspect of humble leadership. He always sought to benefit those around him, embodying the principle that true leadership is about serving others.

Practical Application

Leaders today can practice humility by:

Acknowledging Contributions: Recognise and appreciate the efforts and achievements of team members. This fosters a culture of gratitude and motivates employees.

Seeking Feedback: Encourage and welcome feedback from all levels within the organisation. This not only improves processes but also shows that leaders value others' perspectives.

Leading by Example: Demonstrate humility through actions. Engage in tasks alongside your team and show that no job is beneath you.

Patience is the capacity to endure delays, challenges, and adversity without becoming frustrated or upset. In leadership, patience allows for thoughtful decision-making, fosters a calm work environment, and helps in navigating crises effectively.

Prophetic Example of Patience

Prophet Muhammad (PBUH) exhibited immense patience throughout his life, particularly in the face of persecution and hardship. His patience was rooted in his trust in Allah and his understanding of the bigger picture.

Persecution in Mecca

For over a decade, the Prophet and his followers endured severe persecution in Mecca. Despite the hardships, he remained patient and steadfast, continuing to preach the message of Islam. His patience was a source of strength and inspiration for his followers, showing them the importance of endurance in the face of adversity.

The Ta'if Incident

When the Prophet travelled to Ta'if to seek support, he was met with hostility and violence. The townspeople stoned him, causing severe injuries. Despite this, he did not curse them or seek revenge. Instead, he prayed for their guidance, showing incredible patience and compassion.

The Migration to Medina

The journey to Medina, known as the Hijra, was a challenging and perilous undertaking. The Prophet's patience and strategic planning were crucial in ensuring the safety of his followers. His patience during this period laid the foundation for the establishment of a strong and supportive Muslim community in Medina.

> *"And be patient, for indeed, Allah does not allow to be lost the reward of those who do good." (Quran 11:115)*

This verse emphasises the virtue of patience and its rewarding nature, highlighting the importance of enduring hardships with grace and faith.

Practical Application

Leaders today can cultivate patience by:

Practising Mindfulness: Engage in mindfulness and stress-relief practices that enhance emotional regulation and calmness.

Developing Long-term Vision: Focus on long-term goals rather than immediate results. This helps in maintaining patience during setbacks.

Encouraging a Supportive Environment: Foster a workplace culture that values patience and supports employees during stressful times.

The Power of Resilience in Leadership

Resilience is the ability to recover from setbacks, adapt to change, and keep going in the face of adversity. Resilient leaders are not easily discouraged by challenges and can inspire their teams to stay focused and determined.

The life of Prophet Muhammad (PBUH) is a testament to resilience. Despite numerous challenges, including battles, betrayals, and personal losses, he remained steadfast in his mission. His resilience was fuelled by his faith and unwavering commitment to his cause.

The Battle of Uhud

The Battle of Uhud was a significant setback for the Muslims, resulting in heavy losses. Despite the defeat, the Prophet (PBUH) did not waver in his resolve. He reassessed the situation, learned from the mistakes, and continued to lead his followers with renewed determination.

The Year of Sorrow

In the same year, the Prophet faced immense personal losses, including the death of his beloved wife Khadijah and his uncle Abu Talib. These losses deeply affected him, but he remained resilient, continuing to fulfil his mission with strength and perseverance.

Practical Application

Leaders today can build resilience by:

Embracing Change: View change as an opportunity rather than a threat. Adaptability is key to resilience.

Maintaining Optimism: Cultivate a positive outlook, even in challenging times. This attitude can inspire and uplift the team.

Learning from Failure: Treat failures as learning experiences. Analyse what went wrong, make necessary adjustments, and move forward with renewed determination.

Integrating These Qualities in Leadership

Integrating humility, patience, and resilience into leadership practices can significantly impact an organisation's culture and success. Here are some strategies for leaders to incorporate these traits:

Personal Reflection: Regularly reflect on your leadership style and behaviour. Identify areas where you can be more humble, patient, or resilient. Personal growth in these areas can lead to more authentic and effective leadership.

Training and Development: Invest in training programs that focus on emotional intelligence, stress management, and resilience building. Encourage continuous learning and personal development for yourself and your team.

Lead with Empathy: Empathy is closely linked with humility and patience. Understanding and addressing the needs and concerns of your team fosters a supportive environment. Listen actively, show compassion, and provide support when needed.

Foster a Resilient Culture: Encourage a culture where resilience is valued. Share stories of overcoming adversity, recognise efforts to push through challenges, and provide resources to help employees manage stress and bounce back from setbacks.

Balance Authority with Approachability: Maintain the balance between being an authoritative figure and being approachable. This balance fosters respect and openness, encouraging team members to seek guidance and share their ideas without fear.

Inspiring Others Through Actions

Demonstrating dedication and commitment to organisational goals

Leadership is as much about action as it is about vision. Demonstrating dedication and commitment to organisational goals through one's actions can inspire and motivate teams, fostering a culture of excellence and shared purpose.

By consistently embodying the values and objectives of the organisation, leaders can set a powerful example that encourages others to follow suit.

The teachings of Islam and the exemplary leadership of the Prophet Muhammad (PBUH) provide valuable insights into how leaders can inspire their teams through dedicated and committed actions.

The Power of Leading by Example

Leading by example is a fundamental aspect of effective leadership. When leaders show their commitment to their organisation's goals through their actions, it instils confidence and motivation within their teams.

This approach creates a sense of shared responsibility and encourages employees to align their efforts with the organisation's vision.

Prophet Muhammad (PBUH) exemplified leading by example in every aspect of his life. He was known for his unwavering dedication to his mission, whether through his tireless efforts in spreading the message of Islam, his participation in battles, or his personal conduct in everyday life.

> *"Indeed, in the Messenger of Allah (Muhammad) you have a good example to follow for him who hopes in (the Meeting with) Allah and the Last Day and remembers Allah much." (Quran 33:21)*

This verse highlights the Prophet's role as a model of dedication and commitment for others to emulate.

Demonstrating Dedication and Commitment

Hard Work and Perseverance

Leaders who demonstrate a strong work ethic and perseverance in the face of challenges inspire their teams to adopt the same attitude. This involves being actively involved in projects, showing a willingness to go the extra mile, and maintaining a positive outlook during difficult times.

Prophetic Example: During the construction of the mosque in Medina, Prophet Muhammad (PBUH) worked alongside his companions, carrying bricks and labouring tirelessly. His involvement and hard work set a powerful example for his followers, demonstrating his commitment to their shared goals.

Consistency and Reliability

Consistency in actions and decisions builds trust and reliability. When leaders are consistent in their dedication to organisational goals, it reinforces the importance of these objectives and encourages employees to remain focused and committed.

Prophetic Example: Prophet Muhammad (PBUH) was known for his consistent and reliable leadership. He maintained his principles and values throughout his life, regardless of the circumstances, which earned him the unwavering trust and respect of his followers.

Clear Vision and Communication

A clear vision and effective communication are essential for fostering commitment within a team. Leaders must articulate the organisation's goals clearly and ensure that every team member understands their role in achieving these objectives.

Prophetic Example: The Prophet (PBUH) clearly communicated his vision of a just and moral society based on the principles of Islam. He regularly reminded his followers of their collective goals and the importance of their individual contributions to the larger mission.

Empowering Others

Empowering team members by providing them with the necessary resources, support, and autonomy fosters a sense of ownership and commitment. When employees feel empowered, they are more likely to be dedicated to their tasks and the organisation's goals.

Prophetic Example: The Prophet (PBUH) empowered his companions by delegating responsibilities and trusting them with important tasks. He provided guidance and support but also allowed them the freedom to make decisions and contribute to the mission.

Recognising and Celebrating Achievements

Acknowledging and celebrating the achievements of team members reinforces their commitment and motivates them to continue striving for excellence. Recognition can be in the form of verbal praise, awards, or public acknowledgment of their contributions.

Prophetic Example: Prophet Muhammad (PBUH) frequently praised his companions for their efforts and sacrifices. He recognised their contributions, which boosted their morale and reinforced their commitment to the cause.

Integrating Dedication and Commitment in Leadership Practices

Leading from the Front: Leaders should be visible and active in their efforts to achieve organisational goals. By participating directly in key initiatives and projects, leaders demonstrate their dedication and set a standard for others to follow.

Setting High Standards: Setting high standards for oneself and the team encourages everyone to strive for excellence. Leaders should model the behaviour and performance they expect from their team members.

Continuous Learning and Improvement: Leaders committed to organisational goals should also focus on continuous learning and improvement. This involves staying updated with industry trends, seeking feedback, and encouraging a culture of learning within the team.

Building a Supportive Culture: Creating a supportive and collaborative culture enhances dedication and commitment. Leaders should foster an environment where team members feel valued, supported, and motivated to contribute their best efforts.

Aligning Personal and Organisational Goals: Leaders should align their personal goals with the organisation's objectives. This alignment ensures that their actions are consistently directed towards achieving the organisation's mission and inspires others to do the same.

Practical Application

Consider a scenario where a company is undergoing a major transformation to adopt new technologies. A leader committed to this goal might:

Lead by Example: Actively participate in training sessions and demonstrate a willingness to learn new skills alongside team members.

Communicate Clearly: Regularly update the team on the progress of the transformation, explain the benefits, and outline the steps needed to achieve the goal.

Empower the Team: Provide resources and support for employees to acquire new skills and encourage innovation and experimentation.

Celebrate Milestones: Recognise and celebrate the achievements of individuals and teams who contribute to the transformation, reinforcing their commitment to the change.

Encouraging personal and professional growth among team members

Personal and professional growth are essential for both individuals and organisations. For employees, growth opportunities lead to increased job satisfaction, improved skills, and a greater sense of accomplishment.

For organisations, investing in employee development enhances performance, drives innovation, and reduces turnover. The Quran encourages the pursuit of knowledge and personal growth:

> *"And say, 'My Lord, increase me in knowledge.'" (Quran 20:114)*

This verse highlights the importance of continuous learning and self-improvement, principles that are crucial for both personal and professional development.

Prophet Muhammad (PBUH) emphasised the value of knowledge and personal growth. He encouraged his companions to seek knowledge and develop their skills, recognising that an educated and skilled community was vital for progress.

> "*Seeking knowledge is an obligation upon every Muslim.*" *(Sunan Ibn Majah)*

This hadith underscores the significance of lifelong learning and development for every individual.

Strategies for Encouraging Growth

Providing Learning Opportunities

Offering various learning opportunities is a fundamental way to encourage growth. This can include formal training programs, workshops, seminars, and access to online courses. Leaders should ensure that these opportunities align with both organisational goals and individual interests.

Practical Application: A company can establish a continuous learning program where employees have access to courses related to their field, new technologies, or soft skills development. This not only enhances their capabilities but also keeps them engaged and motivated.

Mentorship and Coaching

Mentorship and coaching provide personalised guidance and support, helping employees navigate their career paths and overcome challenges. Leaders can act as mentors or create mentorship programs that pair experienced employees with those looking to grow.

Prophetic Example: Prophet Muhammad (PBUH) was a mentor to his companions, providing them with guidance, support, and encouragement. He recognised their potential and helped them develop their skills and knowledge.

Practical Application: Implement a mentorship program where senior employees mentor newer or less experienced team members, providing them with advice, support, and feedback on their professional journey.

Encouraging Goal Setting

Setting clear, achievable goals is essential for personal and professional growth. Leaders should work with team members to set individual goals that align with their career aspirations and the organisation's objectives. Regularly reviewing and adjusting these goals ensures continued progress.

Practical Application: Conduct regular goal-setting sessions where employees can discuss their career aspirations and set specific, measurable, achievable, relevant, and time-bound (SMART) goals. Follow up with regular check-ins to review progress and provide support.

Creating a Supportive Environment

A supportive environment is crucial for encouraging growth. Leaders should foster a culture of trust, respect, and open communication, where employees feel safe expressing their ideas, taking risks, and learning from their mistakes.

Practical Application: Promote a culture of feedback where constructive criticism is encouraged, and mistakes are viewed as learning opportunities. Celebrate successes and provide support during setbacks to build resilience and confidence among team members.

Recognising and Rewarding Development

Recognising and rewarding personal and professional growth reinforces the importance of development and motivates employees to continue their efforts. This can be done through formal recognition programs, promotions, or other incentives.

Practical Application: Establish a recognition program that highlights and rewards employees who have demonstrated significant personal and professional growth. This could include awards, public acknowledgements, or financial incentives.

Facilitating Career Advancement

Providing clear pathways for career advancement helps employees see the potential for growth within the organisation. Leaders should ensure that there are opportunities for promotion and career development, based on merit and performance.

Practical Application: Develop a transparent career progression framework that outlines the skills, experiences, and achievements required for advancement within the organisation. Communicate these pathways clearly and support employees in achieving their career goals.

The Importance of Humility in Leadership

Humility is a cornerstone of effective leadership. It is a quality that enables leaders to remain grounded, connected to their followers, and open to learning and growth. While some might mistakenly associate leadership with authority, dominance, or an inflated sense of self, the most successful leaders recognise that humility is essential for fostering collaboration, respect, and long-term success.

The importance of humility in leadership cannot be overstated; it is a virtue that not only enhances a leader's effectiveness but also strengthens the bonds within an organisation, creating an environment where everyone feels valued and empowered.

Humility in leadership is not about diminishing one's strengths or capabilities but about recognising the value and contributions of others. It involves acknowledging that leadership is a shared journey, where the success of the team or organisation is a collective achievement. Leaders who practice humility are more likely to inspire loyalty, encourage innovation, and create a culture of trust and respect.

This comprehensive exploration of the importance of humility in leadership will draw on the life and example of Prophet Muhammad (PBUH), who epitomised humble leadership in every aspect of his life.

Humility in leadership is the ability to balance confidence with modesty, power with gentleness, and authority with a willingness to serve. A humble leader does not seek to elevate themselves above others but instead works to uplift those around them. This quality is essential for building a positive organisational culture, where individuals feel respected, heard, and valued.

A humble leader is one who:

- **Recognises their limitations**: Humble leaders understand that they do not have all the answers and are open to the ideas and expertise of others. They are willing to admit when they are wrong and seek help when needed.

- **Values others' contributions**: Humility involves appreciating and recognising the contributions of others. Humble leaders give credit where it is due and celebrate the successes of their team members.

- **Practices self-reflection**: Humility requires self-awareness and the ability to reflect on one's actions and decisions. Humble leaders regularly assess their behaviour and make adjustments to improve their effectiveness.

- **Encourages a collaborative environment**: Humble leaders foster an environment of collaboration and teamwork, where everyone's input is valued. They encourage open communication and are receptive to feedback.

- **Leads by example**: Humble leaders model the behaviour they expect from others. They demonstrate integrity, fairness, and a commitment to the greater good.

The Impact of Humility on Leadership Effectiveness

Humility is a powerful trait that can significantly enhance a leader's effectiveness. Leaders who embody humility are more likely to build strong, cohesive teams, foster a positive organisational culture, and achieve long-term success. Here are some of the key ways in which humility impacts leadership effectiveness:

Building Trust and Respect

One of the most important outcomes of humble leadership is the development of trust and respect. When leaders demonstrate humility, they show their followers that they are approachable, open to feedback, and genuinely interested in the well-being of others. This fosters a culture of trust, where team members feel comfortable sharing their ideas, concerns, and suggestions without fear of judgment or retribution.

Trust is the foundation of any successful team or organisation. When leaders are humble, they build credibility and earn the respect of their followers. This, in turn, leads to increased loyalty and commitment, as team members are more likely to support a leader they trust and respect. Humble leaders also recognise that trust is a two-way street; they trust their team members to do their jobs effectively and give them the autonomy to take ownership of their work.

The Prophet Muhammad (PBUH) was a prime example of a leader who built trust and respect through humility. Despite his position as the leader of the Muslim community, he lived simply, worked alongside his followers, and always treated others with kindness and respect. His humility endeared him to his companions, who loved and respected him deeply. The trust and loyalty he inspired were key factors in the success of the early Muslim community.

Fostering Collaboration and Teamwork

Humble leaders understand that leadership is not about asserting control but about empowering others to contribute their best. By valuing the input and contributions of all team members, humble leaders create an environment where collaboration and teamwork thrive. They encourage open communication, where everyone's ideas are heard and considered, leading to more innovative and effective solutions.

Collaboration is essential for achieving organisational goals, especially in today's complex and rapidly changing environment. Humble leaders recognise that no one person has all the answers and that the best outcomes are often achieved through collective effort. By fostering a culture of collaboration, humble leaders help their teams achieve more than they could individually.

The Prophet Muhammad (PBUH) consistently demonstrated the importance of collaboration and teamwork. He consulted with his companions on important matters, valued their opinions, and made decisions based on collective input. For example, during the Battle of the Trench, the Prophet sought the advice of his companions, leading to the innovative strategy of digging a trench around Medina, which played a crucial role in the Muslim victory. This approach not only led to successful outcomes but also strengthened the bonds within the community.

Enhancing Learning and Growth

Humility is closely linked to a growth mindset—the belief that abilities and intelligence can be developed through effort, learning, and perseverance. Humble leaders are lifelong learners who are open to new ideas and experiences. They are not afraid to admit their mistakes and view challenges as opportunities for growth rather than threats to their authority.

This openness to learning is a critical component of leadership development. Humble leaders continuously seek to improve themselves and encourage their team members to do the same. By fostering a culture of learning and growth, humble leaders help their organisations adapt to change, innovate, and stay competitive in the long term.

Encouraging Ethical Leadership

Humility is a key component of ethical leadership. Humble leaders are guided by principles of honesty, integrity, and fairness. They are more likely to make decisions that are in the best interest of the organisation and its stakeholders rather than being driven by personal gain or ego. This commitment to ethical leadership helps build a positive organisational culture and enhances the long-term success of the organisation.

Ethical leadership is crucial in today's world, where organisations are increasingly held accountable for their actions by customers, employees, and the broader community. Humble leaders set the tone for ethical behaviour within their organisations by modelling the values they expect from others. They are transparent in their decision-making, take responsibility for their actions, and are committed to doing what is right, even when it is difficult.

The Prophet Muhammad (PBUH) was the epitome of ethical leadership. His humility and commitment to justice and fairness were evident in every aspect of his life. He treated everyone with respect, regardless of their social status, and made decisions that were always in line with the principles of Islam. His ethical leadership inspired his followers to act with integrity and contributed to the establishment of a just and moral society.

Strengthening Resilience and Adaptability

Humility also plays a crucial role in strengthening resilience and adaptability. Humble leaders are better equipped to handle challenges and setbacks because they are willing to acknowledge their limitations and seek help when needed. They do not see failures as a reflection of their worth but as opportunities to learn and improve.

Resilience and adaptability are essential qualities for leaders, especially in times of crisis or rapid change. Humble leaders are more likely to remain calm and composed under pressure, and their willingness to listen to others and adjust their strategies accordingly enables them to navigate difficult situations more effectively.

The Prophet Muhammad (PBUH) demonstrated remarkable resilience and adaptability throughout his life. Despite facing numerous challenges and adversities, he remained steadfast in his mission and adapted his strategies to meet the changing circumstances. His humility allowed him to accept advice from others and make decisions that ensured the survival and growth of the Muslim community.

Prophetic Examples of Humility in Leadership

The life of Prophet Muhammad (PBUH) provides numerous examples of humble leadership. His actions and decisions were always guided by humility, whether he was dealing with his companions, leading his community, or interacting with people from different walks of life. These examples serve as powerful lessons for leaders today, highlighting the impact of humility on effective leadership.

The Prophet's Humble Lifestyle

Despite his status as the leader of the Muslim community, the Prophet Muhammad (PBUH) lived a simple and humble life. He did not seek luxury or material wealth, and he was content with the basic necessities. The Prophet's humility was reflected in his daily habits—he mended his own clothes, milked his goats, and participated in household chores. He never placed himself above others and always treated everyone with kindness and respect.

This humble lifestyle earned the Prophet the love and admiration of his companions and followers. His actions demonstrated that true leadership is not about wealth or status but about serving others and living in accordance with one's values. The Prophet's humility inspired those around him to live modestly and to focus on what truly mattered—faith, character, and service to others.

The Prophet's Response to Praise

The Prophet Muhammad (PBUH) was often praised by his companions and followers for his wisdom, leadership, and character. However, the Prophet always responded to praise with humility, redirecting the praise to Allah and reminding others that he was merely a servant of Allah.

> *For example, when a man once addressed him as "our lord" (sayyiduna), the Prophet immediately corrected him, saying, "The true Lord is Allah alone" (Muslim)*

The Prophet's humility in accepting praise is a powerful reminder that true leadership is not about seeking accolades or recognition but about serving others and fulfilling one's responsibilities with sincerity and devotion.

The Prophet's Interaction with the Poor and Marginalised

One of the most striking examples of the Prophet's humility was his treatment of the poor and marginalised members of society. Despite his status as a leader, he never distanced himself from those who were less fortunate. Instead, he made it a point to engage with them, listen to their concerns, and treat them with the same respect and kindness that he showed to everyone else.

The Prophet would often visit the sick, feed the hungry, and spend time with those who were neglected by society. He would sit with the poor and share meals with them, showing that he valued their company and respected their dignity. His humility in these interactions broke down social barriers and created a sense of inclusion and community.

One notable example is the incident involving an elderly woman who regularly threw trash in the Prophet's path as he walked by her house. When she fell ill and was unable to continue this act, the Prophet noticed her absence and inquired about her well-being. Upon learning that she was sick, he visited her to offer his help. This act of kindness and humility surprised the woman, leading her to embrace Islam. The Prophet's ability to forgive and show compassion, even to those who treated him poorly, exemplifies his humility and commitment to treating all people with respect.

The Prophet's Approach to Leadership During the Construction of the Mosque in Medina

When the Prophet Muhammad (PBUH) and his followers migrated to Medina, one of the first tasks they undertook was the construction of a mosque, which would serve as the centre of the Muslim community. Despite his leadership role, the Prophet did not simply delegate the work to others. Instead, he actively participated in the construction, carrying bricks, digging the ground, and working alongside his companions.

The Prophet's involvement in the physical labour of building the mosque was a powerful demonstration of humility. It showed that he did not consider himself above manual work and that he was willing to contribute to the community's efforts in a tangible way. This act of humility inspired his companions to work harder and reinforced the idea that true leadership involves serving others rather than seeking to be served.

This example also highlights the Prophet's understanding that leadership is not about titles or positions but about action and participation. By working alongside his followers, he fostered a sense of unity and shared purpose, which was crucial in the early days of the Muslim community in Medina.

The Prophet's Response to Personal Attacks and Insults

The Prophet Muhammad (PBUH) faced numerous personal attacks and insults throughout his life, particularly during the early years of his prophethood in Mecca. Despite these provocations, the Prophet consistently responded with humility, patience, and forgiveness, rather than retaliating or seeking revenge.

One example of this is the story of Ta'if. After being rejected by the people of Mecca, the Prophet travelled to the city of Ta'if in hopes of finding support for his mission. However, he was met with hostility and was driven out of the city by a mob that pelted him with stones, causing him physical harm. Despite this cruel treatment, the Prophet did not curse the people of Ta'if or seek revenge. Instead, he prayed for their guidance, asking Allah to bring forth from their descendants those who would worship Him.

This incident is a profound example of the Prophet's humility in the face of personal attacks. His response demonstrated his deep commitment to his mission and his unwavering belief in the power of patience and forgiveness. The humility he showed in this situation eventually bore fruit, as many years later, the people of Ta'if embraced Islam.

The Prophet's Attitude Towards Wealth and Power

The Prophet Muhammad (PBUH) had the opportunity to amass great wealth and power during his lifetime, particularly after the establishment of the Islamic state in Medina and the subsequent victories in battles. However, he chose to live a life of simplicity and humility, avoiding the trappings of wealth and luxury.

The Prophet's personal belongings were few and modest, and he often gave away whatever wealth he had to those in need. He lived in a simple home, wore plain clothes, and slept on a mat made of palm fibres. Even as the leader of a growing community, he continued to live as he had before, focusing on his spiritual responsibilities rather than material possessions.

This humility in the face of wealth and power was a clear message to his followers that true success and fulfilment come not from worldly gains but from spiritual and moral integrity. The Prophet's refusal to indulge in luxury and his commitment to sharing with others set a powerful example of how leaders should approach wealth and authority—with responsibility, generosity, and humility.

The Prophet's Conduct During the Conquest of Mecca

The conquest of Mecca is one of the most significant events in the life of the Prophet Muhammad (PBUH) and the history of Islam. After years of persecution and conflict, the Prophet returned to Mecca with a large army, effectively bringing the city under Muslim control. However, rather than seeking revenge against those who had wronged him and his followers, the Prophet chose the path of forgiveness and humility.

When he entered Mecca, the Prophet did so with his head bowed in humility, acknowledging that the victory was a blessing from Allah, not a personal triumph. He declared a general amnesty, forgiving even his most bitter enemies and ensuring that no blood would be shed. This act of humility and mercy had a profound impact on the people of Mecca, many of whom embraced Islam as a result.

The Prophet's conduct during the conquest of Mecca is a powerful example of how humility can transform victory into an opportunity for reconciliation and peace. By choosing forgiveness over retribution, the Prophet demonstrated that true leadership is about guiding others towards righteousness and unity, rather than seeking personal glory.

The Prophet's Interaction with Non-Muslims

The Prophet Muhammad (PBUH) showed great humility and respect in his interactions with non-Muslims, even those who opposed him. He treated them with fairness, kindness, and justice, recognising their rights and engaging with them in a spirit of mutual respect.

One example of this is the Prophet's interaction with the delegation of Christians from Najran. When they visited Medina to discuss matters of faith, the Prophet welcomed them into his mosque, engaged in respectful dialogue, and allowed them to perform their prayers in the mosque. This gesture of humility and hospitality was unprecedented and demonstrated the Prophet's commitment to peaceful coexistence and respect for religious diversity.

Another example is the Prophet's treatment of the Jewish tribes in Medina. Despite the political tensions and conflicts that arose, the Prophet upheld the rights of the Jewish community and treated them with justice. He ensured they were protected under the Constitution of Medina and their rights to practice their religion were respected. The Prophet's humility in dealing with non-Muslims set a precedent for how Muslims should interact with people of other faiths—with respect, fairness, and compassion.

The Prophet's Relationship with His Family

Prophet Muhammad (PBUH) was known for his humility in his relationships with his family members. He treated his wives, children, and extended family with love, respect, and consideration, setting an example of how a leader should behave in his personal life.

With his wives, the Prophet was gentle, kind, and understanding. He listened to their concerns, helped with household chores, and showed affection and appreciation for them. He emphasised the importance of treating one's spouse with kindness and respect, famously saying,

> *"The best of you are those who are best to their wives, and I am the best of you to my wives" (Sunan al-Timithy)*

With his children, the Prophet demonstrated humility by spending time with them, playing with them, and teaching them important values. He showed deep affection for his daughters, especially Fatimah, whom he treated with great respect and tenderness. His humility as a father and husband made him a role model for Muslim men and reinforced the importance of humility and kindness in family relationships.

The Prophet's humility extended to his grandchildren as well. He would play with them, carry them on his shoulders, and allow them to interrupt his prayers. This behaviour demonstrated his deep love for his family and his understanding that leadership includes being a loving and attentive family member.

Humility is a powerful and essential quality in leadership. It enables leaders to build trust, foster collaboration, and create a positive and inclusive organisational culture. The life of Prophet Muhammad (PBUH) offers profound examples of humble leadership, from his simple lifestyle to his interactions with others and his willingness to forgive even his greatest enemies.

Chapter Eight

Building and Nurturing Relationships

Trust and respect are the bedrock of strong relationships. When people feel valued and respected, they engage deeply and commit wholeheartedly to shared goals. In business, this translates to stronger partnerships and more effective collaborations. By creating an environment where trust is paramount, leaders inspire loyalty and dedication among employees, partners, and stakeholders.

Prophet Muhammad (PBUH) understood the power of trust and respect. His interactions were always marked by genuine care and consideration. Whether dealing with close companions or strangers, he made everyone feel valued and heard. This approach built unwavering trust and deep respect among his followers, fostering a sense of unity and commitment.

Consider the Prophet's approach to forming alliances and friendships. He sought connections not for personal gain but to build a community based on shared values and mutual support. This authenticity made his relationships strong and lasting. In today's business context, leaders can learn from this by approaching networking with integrity. Focusing on how to support and uplift others builds networks that are resilient and grounded in trust and loyalty.

Authentic relationships are built on trust, respect, integrity, and a genuine desire to connect with others. Prophet Muhammad (PBUH) showed that treating others with empathy and sincerity builds strong, supportive networks that endure over time. Imagine a leader who understands their team's needs, communicates openly and honestly, and consistently acts with integrity. Such a leader inspires confidence and loyalty, creating a work environment where everyone feels valued and respected.

In today's fast-paced world, it's easy to overlook the importance of building meaningful relationships. However, the Prophet's example reminds us that true success lies in the connections we make and the impact we have on others. By nurturing relationships based on trust and respect, leaders create a lasting legacy of positive change.

Strengthening Relationships Using Trust and Respect

Cultivating strong partnerships and alliances in business

The Quran, in its divine wisdom, underscores the importance of trust and honesty in all dealings. One poignant verse reminds believers of their duties:

> *"O you who have believed, do not betray Allah and the Messenger or betray your trusts while you know [the consequence]." (Quran 8:27)*

This verse serves as a divine mandate, urging Muslims to uphold their trusts and remain steadfast in their integrity. Betrayal and dishonesty are explicitly condemned, emphasising that trustworthiness is not just a moral choice but a religious obligation. The concept of trust in the Quran is comprehensive, covering personal relationships and societal responsibilities. Trust is seen as a sacred duty, an amanah, that one must fulfil diligently.

Another verse reinforces the importance of fulfilling commitments:

> *"And fulfil [every] commitment. Indeed, the commitment is ever [that about which one will be] questioned."* (Quran 17:34)

This verse highlights the gravity of honouring agreements and commitments, reinforcing the idea that integrity is central to faith. In a business context, this means that promises, contracts, and agreements must be upheld with the utmost sincerity. The Quran's emphasis on honesty and trust creates a moral framework that guides Muslims to conduct their affairs with integrity, fostering a climate of trust and respect in all interactions.

Prophetic Examples

Prophet Muhammad (PBUH) embodied these Quranic principles in every facet of his life, particularly in his business dealings. Renowned as "Al-Amin" (the Trustworthy), his reputation was built on unwavering honesty, fairness, and respect for others. His integrity was such that even before his prophethood, people entrusted him with their valuables and sought his judgment in disputes.

The Business Partnership with Khadijah

One remarkable example from his life is his partnership with Khadijah (may Allah be pleased with her). When she hired him to manage her trading caravan, she received reports of his exceptional honesty and skill, leading her to propose marriage. This partnership, founded on mutual respect and trust, became a cornerstone of his early life and mission. His fair dealings and transparent practices earned him widespread respect, setting a high standard for ethical conduct in business.

The Incident with the Trust

A significant incident highlighting the Prophet's trustworthiness occurred when the Meccans, despite their hostility towards him, still entrusted him with their valuables.

Even as he prepared to migrate to Medina, the Prophet ensured these trusts were returned to their rightful owners. This act of integrity underlines the profound respect and trust he commanded, even from his adversaries.

Cultivating Strong Partnerships and Alliances

Building strong partnerships requires a deliberate and consistent effort to establish and maintain trust and respect. Here are key strategies for cultivating robust business relationships:

Open and Honest Communication

Effective communication is the bedrock of any strong partnership. Open and honest communication fosters transparency, builds trust, and ensures that all parties are aligned with the same goals.

Practical Application: Schedule regular meetings with partners to discuss progress, share updates, and address any concerns. Encourage open dialogue and ensure that all voices are heard and valued.

Mutual Benefit and Shared Goals

Successful partnerships are built on mutual benefit and shared goals. When both parties have aligned interests and work towards common objectives, the partnership is more likely to thrive.

Practical Application: Clearly define the goals and expectations of the partnership at the outset. Identify areas of mutual benefit and ensure that both parties are equally invested in achieving the desired outcomes.

Reliability and Consistency

Reliability and consistency in actions and commitments are crucial for building trust. Partners need to know that they can depend on each other to fulfil their promises and meet their obligations.

Practical Application: Deliver on your commitments consistently. If challenges arise, communicate proactively and work collaboratively to find solutions.

Respect and Consideration

Showing respect and consideration for your partners fosters a positive and collaborative relationship. This involves valuing their opinions, acknowledging their contributions, and being sensitive to their needs and concerns.

Practical Application: Practice active listening during discussions and negotiations. Respect cultural and organisational differences, and be considerate in your interactions.

Flexibility and Adaptability

Flexibility and adaptability are essential for navigating the dynamic nature of business relationships. Being open to change and willing to adjust plans helps maintain a strong and resilient partnership.

Practical Application: Be prepared to adapt to changing circumstances and respond constructively to new challenges. Approach negotiations with a flexible mindset and a willingness to find mutually acceptable solutions.

Building Long-Term Alliances

Long-term alliances are built on a foundation of trust and respect that is nurtured over time. Here are additional strategies for developing enduring business relationships:

Investing in the Relationship

Investing time, resources, and effort into the partnership demonstrates your commitment and builds a strong foundation for long-term collaboration.

Practical Application: Organise joint workshops, training sessions, or team-building activities to strengthen the bond between partners. Invest in joint projects that align with both parties' strategic goals.

Celebrating Successes Together

Celebrating successes and milestones together reinforces the partnership and boosts morale. Recognising and appreciating each other's contributions fosters a sense of shared achievement.

Practical Application: Celebrate key milestones and achievements with your partners. Host joint events or recognition ceremonies to acknowledge and reward collaborative efforts.

Addressing Conflicts Constructively

Conflicts are inevitable in any partnership, but how they are handled can make or break the relationship. Addressing conflicts constructively and with respect helps to resolve issues without damaging trust.

Practical Application: Approach conflicts with a problem-solving mindset. Focus on understanding the root cause of the issue and work collaboratively to find a fair and equitable resolution.

Continuous Improvement and Innovation

Encouraging continuous improvement and innovation within the partnership keeps the relationship dynamic and forward-thinking. Regularly review and refine the partnership to ensure it remains relevant and effective.

Practical Application: Set up regular review meetings to assess the partnership's progress and identify areas for improvement. Encourage brainstorming sessions to generate new ideas and opportunities for collaboration.

Long-Term Vision and Strategic Alignment

Aligning the partnership with a long-term vision and strategic goals ensures that both parties are working towards sustainable success. This alignment helps to maintain focus and drive long-term value.

Practical Application: Develop a shared strategic plan outlining the partnership's long-term vision. Regularly revisit and update this plan to ensure continued alignment and relevance.

Networking with integrity and sincerity

Networking is a crucial component of professional success. It involves building relationships that can provide mutual benefits, such as knowledge sharing, business opportunities, and career advancement. However, the quality of these relationships is significantly influenced by the principles of integrity and sincerity.

Networking with integrity and sincerity means building connections based on honesty, trust, and genuine interest, rather than merely transactional benefits. This approach not only enhances the quality of the network but also ensures long-term, fruitful relationships.

Drawing from Islamic teachings and the example of Prophet Muhammad (PBUH), we can explore how to effectively network with integrity and sincerity.

Integrity is the foundation of any strong relationship. It involves being honest, transparent, and ethical in all interactions. When people trust that you are genuine and reliable, they are more likely to value and reciprocate the relationship.

Prophetic Example

The migration to Medina (Hijra) was a turning point that required establishing new networks in a different environment. Upon arriving in Medina, the Prophet Muhammad (PBUH) immediately worked to build relationships based on mutual respect and support. He established a bond of brotherhood (mu'akhat) between the emigrants (Muhajirun) from Mecca and the helpers (Ansar) of Medina. This bond was more than a political alliance; it was a sincere effort to integrate the community and support each other. The Prophet's genuine approach fostered a sense of unity and trust that was crucial for the survival and growth of the early Muslim community.

Prophet Muhammad (PBUH) also built respectful and sincere relationships with non-Muslims. One notable example is the Charter of Medina, a document that established the rights and duties of all citizens, including Jews and Christians. This charter was a groundbreaking step in creating a pluralistic society where diverse communities could coexist peacefully. The Prophet's respect for different faiths and his fair treatment of all citizens demonstrated his commitment to integrity and justice. These actions helped build a network of allies and supporters beyond the Muslim community.

The Prophet's personal conduct further exemplified his integrity. He was known for his modesty, humility, and genuine concern for others. He would often visit the sick, help the needy, and assist with community tasks, regardless of the person's status. His sincerity in these actions built deep trust and respect among those who knew him. For instance, when he borrowed money, he ensured it was repaid promptly and often with a little extra as a gesture of goodwill. This personal integrity in his interactions made him a trusted and beloved leader.

Even in dealing with his enemies, Prophet Muhammad (PBUH) displayed remarkable integrity. When the Meccans eventually conquered Mecca, many feared retributions for their past actions against the

Muslims. However, the Prophet declared a general amnesty, saying, "Go, for you are free." This act of mercy and forgiveness, despite having the power to exact revenge, showcased his commitment to justice and compassion. This unprecedented act strengthened his network by transforming former enemies into allies and followers.

The Role of Sincerity in Networking

Sincerity involves a genuine interest in others and a commitment to building meaningful connections. It is about valuing relationships for their own sake, rather than viewing them purely as means to an end.

Genuine Interest

Showing genuine interest in others helps to build deeper, more meaningful connections. People appreciate when their experiences, opinions, and aspirations are acknowledged and valued.

Practical Application: Ask open-ended questions that allow others to share their stories and perspectives. Listen actively and show empathy and understanding.

Building Trust

Trust is built through consistent actions that demonstrate reliability and honesty. Sincere interactions create a foundation of trust that strengthens over time.

Practical Application: Follow through on commitments, be transparent about your intentions, and admit mistakes when they occur. Trust is earned through consistency and authenticity.

Providing Value

Networking should be mutually beneficial. By providing value to others, you create a reciprocal relationship where both parties gain.

Practical Application: Offer help, share resources, or provide support without expecting immediate returns. This creates a sense of goodwill and encourages others to reciprocate.

Strategies for Networking with Integrity and Sincerity

Authentic Engagement

Authentic engagement means being yourself and allowing your true personality to shine through in your interactions. Authenticity fosters trust and makes your connections more genuine.

Practical Application: Share your passions, interests, and goals openly. Be honest about your strengths and areas for improvement. Authenticity attracts like-minded individuals who value your genuine self.

Long-Term Perspective

Networking with a long-term perspective involves building relationships that last, rather than seeking immediate gains. Focus on developing connections that can grow and evolve over time.

Practical Application: Invest time in nurturing relationships. Keep in touch with your network regularly, even when you don't need anything from them. This creates a strong foundation for future collaboration.

Ethical Conduct

Maintaining high ethical standards in all interactions is crucial for building a reputable network. Ethical conduct reinforces trust and respect within your network.

Practical Application: Avoid gossip, respect confidentiality, and be fair in all dealings. Uphold your values and principles consistently, even when faced with challenges.

Active Listening

Active listening involves fully concentrating on the speaker, understanding their message, and responding thoughtfully. This practice shows respect and genuine interest in others.

Practical Application: Make eye contact, nod in agreement, and refrain from interrupting. Summarise what the speaker has said to ensure understanding and show that you value their input.

Reciprocity

Reciprocity is the mutual exchange of benefits and support. It ensures that networking relationships are balanced and equitable.

Practical Application: Be willing to give as much as you receive. Offer your help and support whenever possible, and graciously accept assistance when it is offered to you.

Serving the Community and Stakeholders

Contributing to social welfare and community development initiatives

Social welfare and community development are essential components of a holistic approach to business. These efforts help address social issues, improve the quality of life for community members, and contribute to the overall well-being of society. Companies that invest in these areas demonstrate their commitment to being responsible corporate citizens, which can lead to numerous benefits, including enhanced brand loyalty, employee satisfaction, and long-term business sustainability.

The Quran emphasises the importance of helping others and contributing to the welfare of society. It highlights that acts of charity and social welfare are not just virtuous but multiply in their rewards:

> "The example of those who spend their wealth in the way of Allah is like a seed [of grain] that sprouts seven ears; in every ear are a hundred grains. And Allah multiplies [the reward] for whom He wills. And Allah is all-Encompassing and Knowing." (Quran 2:261)

This verse beautifully illustrates the concept of exponential growth in rewards for charitable actions. It likens the act of giving to planting a seed, which not only grows but multiplies many times over, benefiting countless others. This imagery underscores the idea that contributions to social welfare have far-reaching and lasting impacts, much like a single seed can eventually lead to a bountiful harvest. In the context of business, this means that investments in social welfare can yield substantial returns in terms of community goodwill, brand loyalty, and societal improvement.

> "And whatever you spend in good – it will be fully repaid to you, and you will not be wronged." (Quran 2:272)

This verse reassures believers that any good they do will be rewarded, reinforcing the idea that contributing to the welfare of others is both a moral duty and a wise investment. It suggests that the benefits of such actions extend beyond this life, promising divine recompense for efforts made in the pursuit of social good.

Prophetic Example

Prophet Muhammad (PBUH) was deeply committed to social welfare and community development. His actions and teachings consistently emphasised the importance of caring for the needy and improving the community's well-being. He lived by the principle that the best among people bring the most benefit to others.

One profound example of his commitment to social welfare is the establishment of the institution of Zakat. Zakat, one of the Five Pillars of Islam, is a mandatory form of charity designed to redistribute wealth within the Muslim community. It ensures that the rich contribute a portion of their wealth to those in need, thereby fostering economic equity and social cohesion. The practice of Zakat demonstrates a structured approach to social welfare, reflecting the Prophet's vision of a society where the well-being of each member is interconnected with the collective good.

Prophet Muhammad (PBUH) also encouraged voluntary charity (Sadaqah) beyond the obligatory Zakat. He believed that acts of kindness, no matter how small, had significant value. His teachings included practical advice on helping others—from feeding the hungry to caring for orphans. One notable example is the story of the woman who was known for her kindness to animals. The Prophet praised her, stating that her actions towards a thirsty dog earned her Allah's forgiveness and paradise. This narrative highlights the broad scope of social welfare in Islamic teachings, extending compassion and care to all of Allah's creations.

Another significant example is the Charter of Medina, an agreement crafted by the Prophet to govern the city of Medina after his migration from Mecca. The charter was groundbreaking in its emphasis on social justice, mutual assistance, and community welfare. It guaranteed the rights of all citizens, regardless of their faith, and established a framework for coexistence and cooperation. This document exemplified the Prophet's forward-thinking approach to community development, aiming to create a harmonious society where everyone's rights and responsibilities were clearly defined and respected.

In his personal life, the Prophet (PBUH) demonstrated an unwavering commitment to social welfare. He often distributed food and wealth to the needy, even if it meant that he and his family lived modestly. He visited the sick, comforted the grieving, and consistently advocated for the rights of the poor and marginalised. His interactions were characterised by deep empathy and a genuine desire to alleviate suffering.

For instance, he once said:

> *"He is not a believer whose stomach is filled while his neighbour goes hungry." (Sunan al-Kubra, Al-Bayhaqi)*

This statement underscores the importance of social responsibility and the moral imperative to ensure the well-being of others.

Strategies for Contributing to Social Welfare and Community Development

Identifying Community Needs

The first step in contributing to social welfare and community development is identifying the community's needs. Understanding the specific challenges and issues faced by the community allows organisations to develop targeted initiatives that effectively address these needs.

Practical Application: Conduct community surveys, engage with local leaders, and collaborate with non-profit organisations to gather insights into the community's most pressing issues. Use this information to develop programs that have a meaningful impact.

Developing and Implementing Initiatives

Once the community's needs have been identified, organisations can develop and implement initiatives to address them. These initiatives can range from educational programs and healthcare services to environmental conservation and economic development projects.

Practical Application: Partner with local schools to provide educational resources and support, sponsor health clinics to offer medical services to underserved populations, or launch environmental sustainability projects to protect natural resources.

Employee Volunteer Programs

Encouraging employees to participate in volunteer programs is an effective way to foster a culture of community service within the organisation. Employee volunteer programs can enhance team cohesion, boost morale, and provide employees with a sense of purpose and fulfilment.

Practical Application: Create a structured volunteer program that includes options like offering employees paid time off to volunteer, organising company-wide volunteer events, and recognising and rewarding employees who actively participate in community service.

Corporate Philanthropy

Corporate philanthropy involves donating financial resources, products, or services to support social welfare and community development initiatives. These contributions can have a significant impact on addressing community needs and enhancing the organisation's reputation as a socially responsible entity.

Practical Application: Allocate a portion of the company's profits to charitable donations, sponsor local non-profit organisations, or provide in-kind donations of products and services to support community projects.

Building Partnerships with Non-Profit Organisations

Collaborating with non-profit organisations can amplify the impact of a company's social welfare and community development efforts. Non-profits often have the expertise, networks, and resources needed to implement effective programs, making them valuable partners in these initiatives.

Practical Application: Form strategic partnerships with non-profit organisations that align with the company's values and mission. Work together to develop and execute programs that address community needs and achieve shared goals.

Measuring and Communicating Impact

Measuring the impact of social welfare and community development initiatives is essential for ensuring their effectiveness and sustainability. Regularly assessing the outcomes of these initiatives allows organisations to make data-driven decisions and continuously improve their efforts. Additionally, communicating the impact of these initiatives helps build transparency and trust with stakeholders.

Practical Application: Develop metrics to evaluate the success of community programs, such as the number of beneficiaries served, improvements in community well-being, and changes in environmental sustainability. Share the results of these assessments with stakeholders through annual reports, social media updates, and community events.

Case Study: Implementing Social Welfare and Community Development Initiatives

Scenario: A mid-sized technology company wants to enhance its social impact and strengthen its ties with the local community. The company decides to focus on education and environmental sustainability as its primary areas of contribution.

Identifying Community Needs: The company conducts a survey and finds that local schools lack access to modern educational resources and that there is a need for more environmental conservation efforts.

Developing and Implementing Initiatives: In response, the company launches two main initiatives. The first is a digital literacy program for local schools, providing students with access to technology and training in digital skills. The second is an environmental project aimed at restoring local parks and promoting sustainable practices within the community.

Employee Volunteer Programs: The company encourages employees to volunteer for both initiatives, offering paid volunteer days and organising group volunteer events. Employees participate in teaching digital skills workshops and helping with park clean-up and tree-planting activities.

Corporate Philanthropy: The company allocates a portion of its profits to fund these initiatives, purchasing laptops for schools and sponsoring the environmental project. Additionally, the company matches employee donations to related causes.

Building Partnerships with Non-Profit Organisations: To enhance the effectiveness of its initiatives, the company partners with a local non-profit that specialises in education and another that focuses on environmental conservation. These partnerships provide additional resources and expertise, ensuring the success of the programs.

Measuring and Communicating Impact: The company develops metrics to measure the success of its initiatives, such as the number of students gaining digital skills and the amount of parkland restored. The company shares these results through annual reports and community events, demonstrating its commitment to social welfare and community development.

Creating Shared Value Through Corporate Social Responsibility (CSR)

Corporate Social Responsibility (CSR) has evolved beyond mere philanthropic activities to become a strategic approach that integrates social and environmental concerns into business operations. The concept of creating shared value through CSR means aligning business success with societal progress. This approach ensures that the activities benefiting the company also contribute positively to society.

Drawing inspiration from Islamic principles and the exemplary leadership of Prophet Muhammad (PBUH), we can explore how companies can create shared value through effective CSR initiatives.

The Concept of Shared Value

Creating shared value involves developing strategies and practices that enhance the competitiveness of a company while simultaneously advancing the economic and social conditions of the communities in which it operates. This concept goes beyond corporate philanthropy by embedding social responsibility into the core business strategy, ensuring that both the company and the community benefit.

Strategies for Creating Shared Value Through CSR

Integrating CSR into Core Business Strategy

For CSR to create shared value, it must be integrated into the core business strategy. This involves identifying areas where the company's business interests align with societal needs and developing initiatives that address both.

Practical Application: A company in the renewable energy sector could focus its CSR efforts on promoting sustainable energy solutions. This approach not only supports the business's core activities but also addresses environmental concerns and promotes sustainability.

Investing in Community Development

Investing in community development projects can create significant shared value. These projects improve the quality of life for community members and create a positive business environment.

Practical Application: A manufacturing company could invest in local education programs, providing scholarships and building schools. This investment would help develop a skilled workforce, benefit the community, and ensure a steady supply of qualified employees for the company.

Enhancing Employee Well-Being

Employee well-being is a critical aspect of CSR. Companies that prioritise the health, safety, and development of their employees create a more motivated and productive workforce.

Practical Application: Implement comprehensive health and wellness programs, offer professional development opportunities, and ensure safe working conditions. These initiatives enhance employee satisfaction and retention, contributing to overall business success.

Environmental Stewardship

Environmental stewardship involves adopting sustainable practices that reduce a company's ecological footprint. This approach not only benefits the environment but also enhances the company's reputation and operational efficiency.

Practical Application: Implementing energy-efficient technologies, reducing waste, and promoting recycling programs are ways a company can demonstrate its commitment to environmental sustainability. These practices can lead to cost savings and a stronger brand image.

Ethical Supply Chain Management

Ensuring the supply chain is managed ethically is crucial for creating shared value. This involves working with suppliers who adhere to ethical labour practices and environmental standards.

Practical Application: A retail company can audit its suppliers to ensure they meet ethical standards, provide fair wages, and operate sustainably. This approach promotes fair labour practices and environmental responsibility throughout the supply chain.

Benefits of Creating Shared Value Through CSR

Enhanced Reputation and Brand Loyalty

Companies that engage in CSR activities build a positive reputation and foster brand loyalty. Consumers are increasingly looking to support businesses that demonstrate a commitment to social and environmental responsibility.

Practical Application: Regularly communicate CSR achievements through marketing campaigns, annual reports, and social media. Transparency and accountability in CSR efforts build trust and loyalty among customers.

Increased Employee Engagement and Retention

CSR initiatives focusing on employee well-being and development lead to higher levels of engagement and retention. Employees are more likely to remain with a company that values their contributions and invests in their growth.

Practical Application: Involve employees in CSR activities, such as volunteer programs and community projects. This involvement fosters a sense of pride and ownership, enhancing job satisfaction and loyalty.

Improved Risk Management

CSR can help companies identify and mitigate risks related to social and environmental issues. Proactively addressing these risks reduces the potential for negative impacts on the business.

Practical Application: Conduct regular risk assessments to identify potential social and environmental risks. Develop and implement strategies to mitigate these risks, ensuring the company operates responsibly and sustainably.

Long-Term Sustainability

By aligning business success with societal progress, companies ensure their long-term sustainability. CSR initiatives that address social and environmental challenges contribute to a stable and prosperous business environment.

Practical Application: Develop long-term CSR goals that align with the company's strategic vision. Regularly review and update these goals to ensure they remain relevant and impactful.

Case Study: Implementing Shared Value CSR Initiatives

Scenario: A technology company aims to create shared value through its CSR initiatives. The company focuses on digital education and environmental sustainability.

Integrating CSR into Core Business Strategy: The company develops a digital literacy program for underserved communities, providing access to technology and training. This initiative aligns with the company's expertise and addresses the digital divide.

Investing in Community Development: The company partners with local schools to implement the digital literacy program, improving educational outcomes and creating future employment opportunities.

Enhancing Employee Well-Being: The company introduces a wellness program that includes health screenings, fitness classes, and mental health support, promoting a healthy and engaged workforce.

Environmental Stewardship: The company commits to reducing its carbon footprint by adopting renewable energy sources and implementing energy-efficient practices in its operations.

Ethical Supply Chain Management: The company audits its suppliers to ensure they adhere to ethical labour and environmental standards, promoting sustainability throughout its supply chain.

Patience and Forgiveness in Sustaining Relationships

In the tapestry of human relationships, patience and forgiveness are two of the most essential threads. These virtues not only sustain and strengthen relationships but also create an environment where trust, love, and mutual respect can flourish.

Whether in personal, professional, or communal contexts, relationships face challenges, misunderstandings, and conflicts. How we respond to these inevitable hurdles largely determines the quality and longevity of our relationships. Patience and forgiveness, when practised sincerely, can transform difficult situations into opportunities for growth and deeper connection.

Patience allows us to endure difficulties without resorting to anger or frustration, while forgiveness enables us to let go of resentment and move forward with a clean heart. Together, these qualities lay the foundation for healthy, enduring relationships. The life of Prophet Muhammad (PBUH) provides numerous examples of how patience and forgiveness can be practised in relationships, offering timeless lessons for us all.

Patience, or "sabr" in Arabic, is often defined as the ability to endure hardships, delays, or provocation without losing temper or becoming frustrated. In the context of relationships, patience involves being tolerant and understanding of others' shortcomings, differences, and mistakes. It requires a level of emotional maturity that allows individuals to remain calm and composed even in the face of provocation or disappointment.

The Role of Patience in Building Strong Relationships

Patience is crucial in building strong relationships because it helps prevent minor issues from escalating into major conflicts. Misunderstandings and disagreements are inevitable in any relationship, whether between family members, friends, colleagues, or spouses. Without patience, these small issues can quickly spiral out of control, leading to resentment and estrangement.

When we practice patience, we give ourselves and others the space to express our feelings and thoughts without fear of judgment or anger. This openness fosters trust and respect, allowing more effective communication and problem-solving. Patience also enables us to see beyond the immediate discomfort or frustration, helping us to focus on the bigger picture and the long-term health of the relationship.

The Prophet's Example of Patience in Relationships

Prophet Muhammad (PBUH) exemplified patience in all his relationships, whether with his family, companions, or even those who opposed him. His ability to remain calm and composed in the face of provocation and adversity is a testament to his deep inner strength and commitment to maintaining harmonious relationships.

One of the most famous examples of the Prophet's patience is his relationship with his uncle, Abu Talib. Although Abu Talib did not accept Islam, he was a staunch protector of the Prophet and supported him throughout his mission. The Prophet's patience in dealing with his uncle's refusal to embrace Islam is a powerful lesson in maintaining respect and love even when there are significant differences in belief.

Another example of the Prophet's patience is seen in his dealings with the Bedouins, who were often rough in their manners and behaviour. On one occasion, a Bedouin man grabbed the Prophet's cloak roughly, leaving marks on his neck, and demanded that the Prophet give him some of the wealth of the Muslims. Instead of responding angrily, the Prophet smiled, ordered the man to be given what he asked for, and advised him to be gentle in his requests. This incident demonstrates the Prophet's remarkable patience and ability to respond to rudeness with kindness and understanding.

The Importance of Forgiveness in Relationships

Forgiveness is the act of letting go of resentment, anger, and the desire for revenge after someone has wronged us. In relationships, forgiveness is essential for healing and moving forward after conflicts or misunderstandings. Without forgiveness, relationships can become mired in bitterness and negativity, making it difficult to rebuild trust and intimacy.

Forgiveness has a profound healing power, both for the individual who forgives and for the relationship as a whole. When we hold onto grudges or resentment, we carry a heavy emotional burden that can affect our mental and physical well-being. Forgiveness allows us to release this burden, freeing ourselves from the negative emotions that can poison our hearts and minds.

In relationships, forgiveness helps to restore trust and repair the emotional bonds that may have been damaged by a conflict or hurtful behaviour. It opens the door to reconciliation and creates a pathway for rebuilding the relationship on a stronger foundation. Forgiveness does not mean condoning the wrong that was done, nor does it require forgetting the incident. Instead, it involves a conscious decision to let go of the anger and resentment and to focus on the positive aspects of the relationship.

Prophetic Examples of Forgiveness in Relationships

Prophet Muhammad (PBUH) was known for his exceptional capacity to forgive, even in situations where he had been deeply wronged. His forgiveness was not only a reflection of his character but also a means of fostering peace and reconciliation in the community.

One of the most profound examples of the Prophet's forgiveness is his response to the people of Ta'if. After being rejected by the people of Mecca, the Prophet travelled to Ta'if to seek support for his mission. However, the people of Ta'if not only rejected him but also mocked him and drove him out of the city by pelting him with stones, causing him to bleed. Despite this cruel treatment, the Prophet did not seek revenge. Instead, he prayed for their guidance, asking Allah to bring forth from their descendants those who would worship Him. This act of forgiveness and patience exemplifies the Prophet's commitment to peace and his refusal to allow personal grievances to hinder his mission.

Another example of the Prophet's forgiveness is the conquest of Mecca. After years of persecution and conflict, the Prophet returned to Mecca with a powerful army. Despite having the power to exact revenge on those who had wronged him and his followers, the Prophet chose to forgive the people of Mecca. He declared a general amnesty, saying, "Go, for you are free."

This act of forgiveness not only prevented further bloodshed but also paved the way for the peaceful spread of Islam throughout the Arabian Peninsula. The Prophet's ability to forgive his enemies at the height of his power is a powerful lesson in the importance of forgiveness in leadership and relationships.

The Interplay of Patience and Forgiveness

Patience and forgiveness are closely intertwined virtues that reinforce each other in sustaining relationships. Patience provides the emotional resilience needed to endure the hurts and disappointments that inevitably arise in relationships, while forgiveness allows for healing and reconciliation after those hurts have occurred.

Patience as a Pathway to Forgiveness

Patience is often the first step towards forgiveness. When we are patient, we give ourselves time to process our emotions and reflect on the situation before reacting. This pause allows us to move beyond the initial anger or hurt and consider the other person's perspective. It also allows us to weigh the importance of the relationship against the severity of the offence, helping us to determine whether forgiveness is the best course of action.

In many cases, practising patience can prevent conflicts from escalating to the point where forgiveness is needed. By remaining calm and composed, we can address issues before they become major problems, thereby preserving the harmony of the relationship.

Forgiveness as an Expression of Patience

Forgiveness is an expression of patience because it requires us to overcome our immediate emotional reactions and choose a path of compassion and understanding. It is easy to hold onto anger and resentment, but it takes strength and patience to forgive, especially when the offence is serious or deeply personal.

The Prophet Muhammad (PBUH) demonstrated this interplay of patience and forgiveness in many aspects of his life. His patience in enduring hardships and willingness to forgive those who wronged him were key factors in his success as a leader and in the spread of Islam. By practising both patience and forgiveness, the Prophet was able to build strong, lasting relationships that were based on mutual respect and trust.

Chapter Nine

Adaptability and Innovation

Change is inevitable, and the ability to adapt is a hallmark of resilient leadership. Throughout history, leaders who embraced change and showed flexibility in their strategies have consistently achieved remarkable success. Prophet Muhammad (PBUH) exemplified adaptability, showing remarkable foresight and the ability to adjust his approaches to suit different circumstances. His leadership style provides timeless lessons on how to navigate the complexities of change while staying true to core principles.

Prophet Muhammad (PBUH) lived during a time of immense transformation. His ability to read the shifting sands of his environment and respond with wisdom is a testament to his visionary leadership. Whether negotiating the Treaty of Hudaybiyyah or migrating to Medina, he demonstrated a profound understanding of when to stand firm and when to embrace change. This balance between steadfastness and flexibility is a lesson: true leadership lies in knowing when to hold fast to one's principles and when to adapt for the greater good.

Innovation is the engine of progress, propelling businesses forward and opening new avenues for growth. Encouraging creativity within an organisation leads to developing novel solutions and more efficient processes. When teams feel empowered to think outside the box, they contribute to a culture of continuous improvement and breakthrough ideas. This creative spirit, combined with a willingness to embrace technological advancements, positions businesses at the forefront of their industries.

Consider the Prophet's (PBUH) strategy during the Battle of the Trench. When faced with the formidable confederate forces, he adopted the unconventional tactic of digging a trench around Medina, an idea suggested by Salman al-Farsi. This innovative defence strategy, foreign to Arab warfare at the time, proved highly effective and turned the tide of battle. This incident underscores the importance of listening to diverse perspectives and being open to new ideas, no matter how unconventional they may seem.

Technology and digital transformation have revolutionised the way we do business. Leveraging the latest technological tools can significantly enhance efficiency, productivity, and customer satisfaction. Integrating technology with traditional business practices allows for more streamlined operations and better decision-making. However, aligning these advancements with core values and principles is essential to ensure they serve the greater good.

Prophet Muhammad (PBUH) demonstrated how to balance tradition with progress. His ability to integrate new ideas while maintaining foundational values provides a powerful model for modern businesses. One striking example is his approach to governance in Medina. The Constitution of Medina was a pioneering document that outlined the rights and duties of all citizens, regardless of their faith. It was an innovative step towards inclusive governance while firmly rooted in the principles of justice and compassion.

This ability to innovate within the framework of core values is critical for businesses today. As organisations navigate the rapid pace of technological change, they must ensure that their innovations are aligned with their ethical standards and contribute positively to society. This balance between progress and principle creates a sustainable path for growth and success.

Embracing Change and Innovation

Prophetic examples of adaptation and flexibility

Adaptability is the capacity to adjust to new conditions, while flexibility involves the willingness to change or compromise. Together, these qualities enable leaders to navigate uncertainties, respond to challenges, and seize opportunities.

In the business world, organisations that cultivate these traits can innovate more effectively, meet evolving customer needs, and stay ahead of the competition.

The Quran encourages Muslims to reflect, learn, and adapt. This approach to life is integral to achieving personal and collective success. A pertinent verse encapsulates this idea:

> *"And those who listen to the word and follow the best thereof, those are the ones whom Allah has guided, and those are the ones endowed with understanding."* (Quran 39:18)

This verse emphasises the importance of being receptive to new ideas and wisdom. It highlights that true understanding and guidance come from the ability to discern and adopt the best practices and knowledge. The act of listening and then choosing the best course of action reflects a dynamic approach to life, one that values growth and improvement over rigid adherence to the status quo.

This principle is essential for both personal development and organisational growth, advocating for continuous learning and adaptation in response to changing circumstances.

Prophetic Examples of Adaptation and Flexibility

Prophet Muhammad (PBUH) demonstrated remarkable adaptability and flexibility throughout his life. His leadership was characterised by a keen awareness of changing circumstances and a pragmatic approach to addressing them. Here are some notable examples:

The Constitution of Medina

Upon migrating to Medina, Prophet Muhammad (PBUH) found himself in a diverse community consisting of various tribes and faiths. To ensure peaceful coexistence and cooperation, he drafted the Constitution of Medina. This document was a pioneering charter that outlined the rights and responsibilities of all citizens, regardless of their religious affiliations. It established principles of justice, mutual respect, and collective responsibility. By adapting to Medina's social and political realities, the Prophet created a cohesive and inclusive society. This flexibility in governance allowed the nascent Muslim community to thrive and set a model for pluralistic societies.

The Battle of Hunayn

During the Battle of Hunayn, the Muslim army initially faced a significant setback due to an ambush by the enemy. Despite the chaos and confusion, Prophet Muhammad (PBUH) remained steadfast and adapted his strategy in response to the unfolding situation. He regrouped his forces, reinforced their morale, and led a counterattack that ultimately resulted in a decisive victory. This incident highlights the Prophet's ability to remain calm under pressure and adjust his tactics dynamically in response to changing battlefield conditions.

The Economic Boycott

During the early years in Mecca, the Quraysh imposed an economic and social boycott on the Prophet and his followers. This severe hardship required tremendous adaptability and resilience. The Muslim community endured this period by supporting one another, sharing resources, and maintaining their faith. The Prophet's leadership during this crisis involved constant reassurance and practical measures to ensure the community's survival. This period of adversity strengthened the bonds within the Muslim community and showcased their ability to adapt and persevere in the face of extreme challenges.

The Treaty of Hudaybiyyah (Explored Philosophically)

While the Treaty of Hudaybiyyah has been frequently cited, its deeper philosophical insights bear reiteration. This treaty was not just a political manoeuvre but a profound lesson in strategic patience and foresight. The Prophet's willingness to accept seemingly disadvantageous terms demonstrated his deep understanding of the larger picture.

The treaty allowed for a period of peace and stability, which enabled the Muslims to focus on internal growth and spreading their message. The eventual outcome, including the conversion of many Quraysh leaders to Islam, validated the Prophet's foresight. This incident underscores that true adaptability often involves sacrificing short-term gains for long-term benefits.

Encouraging Creativity and Innovation in Business Practices

Building on these prophetic examples, modern leaders can foster creativity and innovation within their organisations by embracing change and promoting a culture of adaptability. Here are some strategies to achieve this:

Cultivating an Open-Minded Culture

Encouraging an open-minded culture where new ideas are welcomed and valued is essential for fostering innovation. Leaders should create an environment where employees feel safe to express their thoughts and experiment with new approaches.

Practical Application: Implement regular brainstorming sessions, innovation workshops, and open forums where employees can share ideas and collaborate on projects. Recognise and reward creative contributions to motivate continued innovation.

Learning from Diverse Perspectives

Embracing diversity in the workplace brings a variety of perspectives and experiences that can spark creativity and innovation. Leaders should actively seek input from team members with different backgrounds and expertise.

Practical Application: Form diverse teams for projects and encourage cross-functional collaboration. Promote inclusivity and ensure that all voices are heard and considered in decision-making processes.

Embracing Technological Advancements

Staying abreast of technological advancements and integrating them into business operations can enhance efficiency, productivity, and competitiveness. Leaders should be proactive in exploring and adopting new technologies that align with their organisational goals.

Practical Application: Invest in training programs to upskill employees on the latest technologies. Pilot new tools and systems to evaluate their effectiveness before full-scale implementation.

Being Agile and Responsive

Agility is the ability to respond quickly and effectively to changes. Leaders should cultivate a mindset of continuous improvement and be willing to pivot strategies when necessary.

Practical Application: Implement agile project management methodologies that allow for iterative development and quick adjustments. Encourage a culture of feedback and continuous learning to stay responsive to market changes.

Aligning Innovation with Core Values

While embracing change and innovation, it is crucial to align new initiatives with the organisation's core values and mission. This ensures that innovation efforts are sustainable and resonate with the company's identity.

Practical Application: Develop a clear innovation strategy that aligns with the organisation's vision and values. Regularly review and adjust this strategy to ensure it remains relevant and impactful.

Case Study: Implementing Adaptability and Innovation in a Modern Company

Scenario: A mid-sized manufacturing company faces increased competition and market volatility. The company's leadership decides to implement a strategy of adaptability and innovation to stay competitive.

Cultivating an Open-Minded Culture: The company introduces regular innovation forums where employees from all departments can present new ideas. Successful ideas are funded and developed further, fostering a culture of creativity.

Learning from Diverse Perspectives: Cross-functional teams are formed for key projects, bringing together employees with different skills and backgrounds. This diversity sparks innovative solutions to complex problems.

Embracing Technological Advancements: The company invests in new manufacturing technologies, such as automation and data analytics, to enhance efficiency and reduce costs. Employees are trained on these technologies to ensure smooth integration.

Being Agile and Responsive: Agile methodologies are adopted for project management, allowing the company to quickly adapt to changes in the market. Regular feedback loops ensure continuous improvement.

Aligning Innovation with Core Values: The company's innovation strategy is closely aligned with its commitment to sustainability. New initiatives are evaluated for their environmental impact, ensuring that innovation supports the company's core values.

Encouraging creativity and innovation in business practices

Creativity and innovation are the lifeblood of progress. They lead to the development of new products, the improvement of processes, and the discovery of more efficient ways to meet customer needs. In business, these elements are essential for:

Competitive Advantage: Innovative companies can differentiate themselves from competitors, offering unique value propositions that attract and retain customers.

Adaptability: Creative thinking allows businesses to quickly adapt to changes in the market and respond to new challenges and opportunities.

Growth: Innovation drives business growth by opening up new markets, improving efficiency, and increasing profitability.

The Quranic View on Creativity and Innovation

The Quran encourages reflection, critical thinking, and the pursuit of knowledge, all of which are foundational to creativity and innovation:

> *"Say, 'Are those who know equal to those who do not know?' Only they will remember [who are] people of understanding." (Quran 39:9)*

This verse underscores the importance of knowledge and intellectual pursuit. It highlights that those who possess understanding and knowledge are better equipped to navigate the complexities of life. In a business context, this translates to fostering a culture where learning, exploration, and creativity are highly valued.

> *"And He has subjected to you whatever is in the heavens and whatever is on the earth, all from Him. Indeed, in that are signs for a people who give thought." (Quran 45:13)*

Here, the Quran invites believers to reflect on the vast resources provided by Allah and to use them wisely. This encouragement to explore and utilise available resources can be seen as a call to innovate and create, using the gifts and opportunities provided by the natural world.

Prophetic Examples of Creativity and Innovation

Prophet Muhammad (PBUH) displayed remarkable creativity and openness to new ideas throughout his life. His leadership was marked by a willingness to adopt novel strategies and approaches, demonstrating the profound impact of creativity and innovation.

The Establishment of the Market in Medina

Upon migrating to Medina, the Prophet (PBUH) recognised the need for an organised economic system to support the growing Muslim community. He established a marketplace that operated on principles of fairness and honesty, setting guidelines to prevent fraud and exploitation. This market became a hub of economic activity and innovation, promoting trade and commerce in an ethical manner. By encouraging entrepreneurship and creating an environment where businesses could flourish, the Prophet demonstrated how structured innovation could lead to prosperity.

The Use of Letters to Foreign Leaders

In a groundbreaking move for his time, Prophet Muhammad (PBUH) sent letters to various foreign leaders, inviting them to Islam and establishing diplomatic relations. This act of reaching out to the wider world was innovative and forward-thinking, showcasing his strategic vision. The Prophet's approach to diplomacy was based on mutual respect and understanding, paving the way for peaceful relations and exchanges of knowledge and culture.

Strategies for Encouraging Creativity and Innovation

Fostering a Culture of Openness and Trust

A culture of openness and trust is essential for encouraging creativity. Employees need to feel safe to express their ideas without fear of ridicule or retribution. This environment fosters free thinking and allows innovative ideas to surface.

Practical Application: Encourage open communication and active listening within the organisation. Create platforms such as suggestion boxes, innovation forums, or regular brainstorming sessions where employees can freely share their ideas.

Providing Resources and Training

Investing in resources and training that support creativity and innovation is crucial. This includes providing access to the latest technologies, tools, and educational opportunities that can inspire new ways of thinking.

Practical Application: Offer workshops, courses, and access to online learning platforms that focus on creativity and innovation. Ensure employees have the tools they need to experiment and develop their ideas.

Encouraging Cross-Functional Collaboration

Cross-functional collaboration brings together diverse perspectives and skills, fostering an environment where innovative ideas can thrive. When people from different departments and backgrounds work together, they can combine their unique insights to solve problems in new ways.

Practical Application: Form cross-functional teams for key projects and encourage regular interaction between different departments. This can be facilitated through joint meetings, collaborative projects, and team-building activities.

Recognising and Rewarding Innovation

Recognition and rewards are powerful motivators for encouraging creativity and innovation. When employees see that their innovative efforts are valued and rewarded, they are more likely to continue contributing new ideas.

Practical Application: Implement a reward system that recognises and celebrates innovative contributions. This can include financial incentives, public recognition, or opportunities for career advancement.

Allowing Time for Creative Thinking

Creativity often requires time and space to flourish. Allocating dedicated time for creative thinking and experimentation can help employees develop and refine their ideas without the pressure of immediate deadlines.

Practical Application: Introduce policies such as "innovation hours" or "creative Fridays," where employees can dedicate time to work on new ideas or personal projects. Encourage a work-life balance that allows for mental rejuvenation and creative thinking.

Integrating Islamic Principles in Encouraging Innovation

Islamic teachings provide a strong ethical framework that can enhance creativity and innovation. By integrating these principles, organisations can foster a culture that values ethical conduct, social responsibility, and continuous improvement.

Upholding Integrity and Ethics

Innovation should be pursued within the bounds of ethical conduct and integrity. This ensures that new ideas and practices benefit society and do not cause harm.

Prophetic Example: Prophet Muhammad (PBUH) emphasised the importance of honesty and ethical conduct in all dealings. His commitment to integrity serves as a model for pursuing innovation responsibly.

Emphasising the Pursuit of Knowledge

Islam encourages the pursuit of knowledge and continuous learning, which are essential for fostering innovation.

Prophetic Example: The Prophet (PBUH) said,

> *"Seeking knowledge is an obligation upon every Muslim." (Sunan Ibn Majah)*

This hadith underscores the value of learning and intellectual growth.

Promoting Social Responsibility

Innovative ideas should aim to benefit society and contribute to the common good. This aligns with the Islamic principle of social responsibility.

Practical Application: Encourage employees to develop solutions that address social and environmental challenges. Support initiatives that have a positive impact on the community and the environment.

Case Study: Implementing Innovation Strategies in a Modern Company

Scenario: A mid-sized technology company aims to foster a culture of creativity and innovation to stay competitive in a rapidly changing industry.

Fostering a Culture of Openness and Trust: The company implements regular innovation forums and brainstorming sessions where employees can share ideas openly. Leadership actively listens and provides feedback, creating an environment of trust and support.

Providing Resources and Training: The company invests in cutting-edge tools and technologies and offers training programs on creativity and innovation. Employees have access to online courses and workshops that inspire new ways of thinking.

Encouraging Cross-Functional Collaboration: Cross-functional teams are formed for key projects, bringing together employees from different departments to collaborate and innovate. Regular joint meetings and team-building activities are organised to foster collaboration.

Recognising and Rewarding Innovation: The company introduces an innovation award that recognises and rewards employees for their creative contributions. Winners receive financial incentives and public recognition, motivating others to innovate.

Allowing Time for Creative Thinking: The company designates "innovation hours" each week, allowing employees to work on personal projects or new ideas without the pressure of immediate deadlines. This time fosters creative thinking and experimentation.

Embracing Technology and Digital Transformation

Leveraging technology to enhance business efficiency and productivity

In the rapidly evolving landscape of modern business, embracing technology and digital transformation has become crucial for enhancing efficiency, productivity, and competitiveness. While the context of Prophet Muhammad's (PBUH) time was vastly different, the underlying principles of adaptability, foresight, and ethical innovation can be applied to contemporary challenges. By drawing on these timeless principles, businesses can navigate the complexities of digital transformation while staying true to their core values.

The Quran emphasises the importance of seeking knowledge and understanding the world, which can be extended to the realm of technological advancement:

> *"He taught man what he did not know." (Quran 96:5)*

This verse highlights the divine encouragement for learning and discovery. It reflects the importance of acquiring new knowledge and skills, which in today's world includes technological proficiency. Embracing new tools and methods to enhance human capabilities is in line with this divine instruction to learn and grow.

Strategies for Leveraging Technology to Enhance Efficiency and Productivity

Automating Routine Tasks

Automation is a cornerstone of digital transformation. By automating routine tasks, businesses can significantly reduce the time and effort required for these activities, leading to increased efficiency and productivity.

Practical Application: Implement software solutions that automate tasks such as payroll processing, inventory management, and customer service. For example, using robotic process automation (RPA) can streamline data entry and processing, freeing up employees to focus on more value-added tasks.

Enhancing Communication and Collaboration

Advanced communication tools facilitate seamless collaboration among team members, regardless of their physical location. This connectivity is crucial for maintaining productivity, especially in remote and hybrid work environments.

Practical Application: Adopt collaboration platforms such as Slack, Microsoft Teams, or Zoom to enable real-time communication and virtual meetings. These tools help teams stay connected, share information quickly, and collaborate effectively on projects.

Utilising Data Analytics and Business Intelligence

Data analytics and business intelligence tools provide insights that can drive strategic decision-making. By analysing data from various sources, businesses can identify trends, measure performance, and make informed decisions.

Practical Application: Implement data analytics platforms such as Tableau, Power BI, or Google Analytics to gather and analyse data. Use these insights to inform business strategies, optimise marketing campaigns, and improve operational efficiency.

Streamlining Workflows

Technology can optimise workflows by integrating various business processes into a single, cohesive system. This integration eliminates bottlenecks and ensures that tasks are completed more efficiently.

Practical Application: Use enterprise resource planning (ERP) systems such as SAP or Oracle to integrate core business processes, including finance, HR, and supply chain management. This holistic approach improves coordination and efficiency across the organisation.

Embracing Cloud Computing

Cloud computing offers flexible, scalable, and cost-effective solutions for managing business operations. By migrating to the cloud, businesses can access resources on demand, reduce IT costs, and enhance data security.

Practical Application: Leverage cloud services from providers like AWS, Microsoft Azure, or Google Cloud to host applications, store data, and run analytics. Cloud computing enables businesses to scale their operations quickly and efficiently.

Integrating Islamic Principles in Embracing Technology

Islamic teachings provide an ethical framework that can guide the responsible use of technology. By integrating these principles, businesses can ensure that their digital transformation efforts are both effective and morally sound.

Promoting Ethical Use of Technology

Technology should be used in ways that benefit society and uphold ethical standards. This includes ensuring data privacy, preventing misuse, and promoting transparency.

Prophetic Example: Prophet Muhammad (PBUH) emphasised honesty and integrity in all dealings. Ensuring ethical use of technology aligns with these values by protecting user data and maintaining transparency.

Encouraging Continuous Learning

The rapid pace of technological advancement requires continuous learning and adaptation. Encouraging a culture of learning ensures that employees stay updated with the latest tools and practices.

Prophetic Example: The Prophet (PBUH) said,

> *"Whoever follows a path in the pursuit of knowledge, Allah will make a path to Paradise easy for him." (Sahih Muslim)*

This hadith underscores the importance of lifelong learning, which is crucial for staying abreast of technological changes.

Fostering Social Responsibility

Technology should be leveraged to create a positive social impact. This includes using technology to address social issues, improve access to education and healthcare, and promote sustainability.

Practical Application: Develop tech-driven initiatives that address community needs, such as online education platforms, telehealth services, or environmental monitoring systems. These efforts align with the Islamic principle of social responsibility and contribute to the common good.

Case Study: Successful Digital Transformation

Scenario: A mid-sized retail company aims to enhance its efficiency and productivity through digital transformation.

Automating Routine Tasks: The company implements an RPA solution to automate inventory management and order processing. This reduces manual errors and speeds up operations, allowing employees to focus on customer service and strategic planning.

Enhancing Communication and Collaboration: The company adopts Microsoft Teams to facilitate communication among its geographically dispersed teams. This platform enables real-time collaboration, file sharing, and virtual meetings, improving overall productivity.

Utilising Data Analytics and Business Intelligence: The company deploys Power BI to analyse sales data, track customer preferences, and identify market trends. These insights inform marketing strategies and inventory decisions, leading to increased sales and customer satisfaction.

Streamlining Workflows: The company integrates its ERP system with its e-commerce platform, ensuring seamless coordination between online sales, inventory management, and shipping. This integration improves order fulfilment speed and accuracy.

Embracing Cloud Computing: The company migrates its IT infrastructure to AWS, reducing IT costs and enhancing data security. The cloud platform provides scalable resources that support the company's growth and innovation efforts.

Integrating Sunnah principles with modern advancements in business

The Sunnah encompasses a wide range of ethical and moral guidelines that are relevant to various aspects of life, including business. These principles include honesty, integrity, fairness, social responsibility, and respect for others. Integrating these values into modern business practices ensures that companies operate ethically and contribute positively to society.

We've already seen how honesty and transparency are foundational to trust and strong reputations in business. These principles, deeply rooted in the Sunnah, translate into modern practices like transparent financial reporting, clear stakeholder communication, and truthful marketing.

Reflecting on these discussions, it becomes evident that transparency goes beyond mere compliance. It's about creating an environment where all stakeholders feel informed and valued. This approach reduces uncertainties and builds a culture of trust. For instance, consider how clear communication during a financial crisis can maintain investor confidence and employee morale. In essence, transparency transforms potential vulnerabilities into strengths by fostering an atmosphere of openness and reliability.

The prophetic example of paying workers promptly underscores a broader commitment to human dignity and respect.

In modern terms, this principle translates into fair labour practices and equitable opportunities for career advancement. The impact is profound: businesses that prioritise fairness often see higher employee satisfaction and retention rates. Fair pricing strategies also enhance customer loyalty. By ensuring all transactions are just, companies build a solid foundation of trust and reliability.

The Sunnah encourages giving back to the community and helping those in need. Businesses have a responsibility to contribute to the well-being of society, transcending the mere pursuit of profit. We've discussed the emphasis on social responsibility and the Prophet's teaching about the significance of caring for one's neighbours. This principle is pivotal in shaping corporate social responsibility (CSR) programs today.

Reflecting on these discussions, we see that genuine community engagement goes beyond charitable donations. It involves actively participating in community development and addressing pressing social issues. Businesses that adopt this approach often find that their social initiatives also drive business success. For example, tech companies offering educational programs not only uplift communities but also build a future talent pool, creating a symbiotic relationship between business growth and social welfare.

Sustainability is a growing concern in modern business, reflecting a broader recognition of our responsibility to the environment. The Sunnah advocates for the responsible use of resources and caring for the environment, principles that are increasingly relevant today.

Prophet Muhammad (PBUH) said:

> *"The world is green and beautiful, and Allah has appointed you as His stewards over it. He sees how you acquit yourselves." (Sahih Muslim)*

This hadith highlights the divine mandate to protect and preserve the natural world, underscoring the importance of environmental stewardship.

Modern businesses can adopt sustainable practices such as reducing waste, conserving energy, and using eco-friendly materials. Implementing policies that minimise the environmental impact of business operations not only fulfils a moral duty but also promotes long-term ecological balance. Sustainable business practices can enhance a company's reputation and ensure compliance with environmental regulations.

Case Study: A Company Integrating Sunnah Principles with Modern Advancements

Consider a mid-sized technology firm aiming to integrate Sunnah principles into its business practices while leveraging modern advancements to enhance efficiency and competitiveness.

The company adopts transparent financial practices, providing clear and accurate reports to stakeholders. It ensures that all advertising is truthful and not misleading, building a reputation for reliability and integrity. By implementing a fair wages policy and non-discriminatory hiring practices, it ensures that all employees are compensated justly and have equal opportunities for career advancement. The firm also establishes a clear and fair grievance resolution process to handle workplace disputes impartially.

Social responsibility is woven into the fabric of the company's operations. They initiate a CSR program focused on technology education for underprivileged youth, providing scholarships and hosting coding workshops. Employees are encouraged to volunteer in community projects, and the company regularly donates a portion of its profits to local charities.

Leadership training programs are introduced, emphasising ethical decision-making and servant leadership. The governance structure includes transparent decision-making processes and accountability measures, ensuring that leaders act in the best interest of both the company and the community.

The firm adopts a comprehensive sustainability policy, incorporating renewable energy sources, reducing waste through recycling programs, and designing products with eco-friendly materials. Regular environmental impact assessments help them continually improve their sustainability practices.

Benefits of Integrating Sunnah Principles with Modern Business Practices

Enhanced Reputation and Trust: By integrating Sunnah principles, businesses can build a strong reputation for ethical behaviour, which fosters trust among customers, employees, and partners. This trust is crucial for long-term success and customer loyalty.

Improved Employee Morale and Retention: Employees who work in a fair and ethical environment are more likely to be satisfied and loyal to the company. Ethical practices and a strong sense of social responsibility can enhance employee morale, leading to higher retention rates and increased productivity.

Positive Social Impact: Businesses that engage in social responsibility initiatives can significantly improve the well-being of their communities. This positive impact not only benefits society but also creates a supportive environment for the business, potentially leading to new opportunities and partnerships.

Long-Term Sustainability: Sustainable business practices ensure that companies can continue to operate successfully without depleting resources or harming the environment. This focus on sustainability is increasingly important in a world where consumers and investors are becoming more environmentally conscious.

Ethical and Effective Leadership: Leaders who embrace ethical principles set a strong example for their teams, promoting a culture of integrity and responsibility. This ethical leadership can drive better decision-making and foster a positive organisational culture.

Chapter Ten

Legacy and Impact

The true measure of a leader's greatness lies not just in their immediate achievements but in the lasting legacy they leave behind. Prophet Muhammad (PBUH) stands as a timeless beacon, illuminating the path for leaders across generations. His leadership, deeply rooted in wisdom, compassion, and integrity, continues to inspire and guides individuals and organisations towards excellence and ethical conduct.

Prophet Muhammad's legacy is a testament to the transformative power of principled leadership. His remarkable ability to unite diverse communities, foster justice and compassion, and uphold unwavering ethical standards has left an indelible mark on the world. Reflecting on his life, we see that the true impact of a leader extends far beyond their lifetime, shaping the values and actions of future generations.

One cannot overlook the profound essence of his leadership style. It was not just about the grand gestures or significant victories, but the everyday acts of kindness, fairness, and wisdom. He led by example, embodying the very principles he preached. This congruence between words and actions created a powerful, lasting impression on those around him. His leadership was a living testament to the values of humility, patience, and resilience.

A crucial aspect of leaving a lasting legacy is the commitment to continuous improvement and learning. Leaders who embrace lifelong learning and personal development not only enhance their own capabilities but also inspire their teams to pursue excellence. This dedication to growth ensures that the principles of ethical leadership are sustained and adapted to meet the evolving challenges of the future. The Prophet's (PBUH) life was a continuous journey of seeking knowledge, adapting to new circumstances, and guiding his followers with wisdom and foresight.

The journey of a leader is one of constant evolution, driven by a deep-seated commitment to making a positive difference. Embracing the teachings of the Sunnah, leaders today can navigate the complexities of modern business with integrity and purpose. The Prophet's adaptability, from his strategic decisions during times of conflict to his innovative solutions in governance, exemplifies how flexibility and foresight are crucial for sustainable leadership.

Leaving a Lasting Legacy Through Leadership

Examining the legacy of Prophet Muhammad (PBUH) in leadership

At the heart of the Prophet's leadership was an extraordinary balance of compassion and justice. His empathy was not merely a sentiment but a driving force behind his every decision. The Prophet's mission, as the Quran states, was to be a mercy to the worlds. This mission manifested in a leadership style that consistently sought to alleviate suffering and promote well-being.

His deep compassion was always intertwined with an unwavering commitment to justice, ensuring that every individual, regardless of their background, was treated with dignity and respect.

The Prophet's approach to justice was not rigid; it was infused with mercy and foresight. During the conquest of Mecca, his decision to forgive his former adversaries was not just an act of mercy but a strategic move to unite a fractured society. This act of clemency underscores a profound understanding that true justice goes beyond retribution; it is about restoring harmony and fostering unity. His wisdom in choosing forgiveness over vengeance highlights a leadership quality that prioritises long-term peace over short-term victories.

Integrity and trustworthiness were pillars of the Prophet's character, earning him the title "Al-Amin," the Trustworthy. This reputation was not built overnight but was the result of a lifetime of honest and fair dealings. His integrity established a foundation of trust that was crucial for uniting diverse communities. The high regard for integrity in leadership is echoed in the hadith:

> *"The truthful and trustworthy merchant is with the Prophets, the truthful, and the martyrs" (Tirmidhi)*

This respect for honesty and reliability created a stable and cohesive society, where people felt secure in their dealings and interactions.

The Prophet's visionary leadership was marked by an exceptional ability to foresee challenges and opportunities. His strategic foresight was evident in the establishment of the Constitution of Medina, which unified diverse tribes under a single framework of justice and mutual respect.

This visionary approach laid the groundwork for a just and inclusive society, showcasing his ability to blend idealism with practical governance. The Prophet's vision was not limited to immediate gains but encompassed long-term societal well-being.

Empowerment and inclusivity were central to the Prophet's leadership philosophy. He recognised the potential in every individual and encouraged active participation in community affairs. His inclusive approach is beautifully encapsulated in the hadith:

> *"The believers, in their mutual kindness, compassion, and sympathy, are just like one body. When one of the limbs suffers, the whole body responds to it with wakefulness and fever" (Sahih Bukhari)*

This principle fostered a sense of solidarity and mutual support, empowering individuals to contribute meaningfully to the community.

Adaptability and innovation were also key traits of the Prophet's leadership. He was open to new ideas and willing to adopt strategies that best served his community's interests. This flexibility is evident in the innovative defensive strategy during the Battle of the Trench. His willingness to embrace new ideas and methods underscores the importance of adaptability in leadership. The Prophet's approach to governance, warfare, and diplomacy was marked by a readiness to innovate while staying true to core principles.

The Prophet's leadership was characterised by a profound understanding of human nature and a deep sense of responsibility towards his followers. He knew true leadership involved serving others, fostering a sense of community, and working towards the common good. This understanding is reflected in his actions and decisions, which were always guided by ethical considerations and a desire to promote justice and compassion.

Reflecting on the legacy of Prophet Muhammad (PBUH), it becomes clear that his leadership principles are as relevant today as they were over fourteen centuries ago. His life teaches us that true leadership is about serving others, fostering trust, and striving for the greater good. His emphasis on moral integrity, social justice, and compassionate governance provides a timeless blueprint for ethical leadership.

The legacy of Prophet Muhammad (PBUH) is a testament to the enduring power of ethical and compassionate leadership. His principles of honesty, justice, inclusivity, and innovation continue to inspire leaders around the world. His example demonstrates that true leadership is not about authority or control but about empowering others and creating a vision that inspires collective effort.

Reflecting on the impact of Sunnah-inspired leadership on organisations and communities

Reflecting on the impact of Sunnah-inspired leadership reveals a transformative power that shapes not just organisations but entire communities. Imagine a leader whose every action is imbued with honesty and integrity, fostering a culture of trust that permeates every level of their organisation. This trust isn't just a fleeting feeling; it's a solid foundation upon which the entire structure stands firm. Such a leader doesn't merely talk about values but lives them, creating a workplace where open communication and collaboration thrive.

Consider the profound wisdom behind the Quranic verse:

> *"O you who have believed, fear Allah and be with those who are true." (Quran 9:119)*

This call to truthfulness echoes through the halls of an organisation, creating an atmosphere where integrity isn't just encouraged but expected. Leaders who embody this principle inspire a ripple effect of trustworthiness, leading to a culture where employees feel safe to express ideas, take risks, and innovate. The result? A resilient organisation that can weather any storm, built on the rock-solid foundation of integrity.

Now, imagine a workplace infused with compassion and inclusivity, where every individual feels seen, heard, and valued. The Prophet Muhammad (PBUH) exemplified this through his life, always prioritising empathy and solidarity. Reflect on the hadith:

> *"The believers, in their mutual kindness, compassion, and sympathy, are just like one body. When one of the limbs suffers, the whole body responds to it with wakefulness and fever." (Sahih Bukhari)*

This principle, when woven into the fabric of an organisation, transforms it into a community where every member feels a deep sense of belonging. Leaders who practice compassion and inclusivity create an environment where morale soars, productivity peaks, and innovation flourishes. Employees, feeling valued and respected, bring their whole selves to work, driving the organisation forward with collective enthusiasm and creativity.

Justice and fairness are the twin pillars that uphold the moral architecture of Sunnah-inspired leadership. Picture a leader who stands firm for justice, even when it's not the easy path.

The Quran calls leaders to transcend personal biases, ensuring that every decision is made with fairness and integrity. In such an organisation, fairness isn't just a policy; it's a way of life. Employees trust that their efforts will be recognised and rewarded equitably, creating a harmonious workplace where disputes are resolved with transparency and respect. This culture of justice fosters loyalty and engagement, reducing turnover and building a strong, committed team.

Envision an organisation where continuous improvement and innovation are more than just buzzwords; they are the lifeblood of the company. Sunnah-inspired leadership encourages a relentless pursuit of knowledge and growth, as captured in the hadith:

> *"Acquire knowledge and impart it to the people." (Al-Tirmidhi)*

This pursuit of knowledge is a spiritual journey, one that leaders embark on with their teams. By fostering a culture of learning and innovation, these leaders ensure their organisations remain dynamic and competitive. Employees are encouraged to think creatively, take risks, and continuously seek better ways to do their work.

This environment not only drives innovation but also personal fulfilment, as employees find joy and purpose in their growth and contributions.

Finally, imagine an organisation deeply embedded in its community, actively engaging in social responsibility and development. Sunnah-inspired leaders extend their impact beyond their organisational walls, embracing their role in societal well-being. Reflect on the hadith:

> *"The best among you are those who have the best manners and character." (Sahih Bukhari)*

Such leaders inspire their organisations to participate in charitable activities, support local initiatives, and implement sustainable practices. These efforts not only enhance the organisation's reputation but also build strong, positive relationships with the community.

This legacy of social responsibility fosters a sense of purpose and pride among employees, who see their work contributing to a greater good.

The long-term impact of Sunnah-inspired leadership is profound and far-reaching. Organisations rooted in these principles achieve sustainable growth, driven by trust, loyalty, and continuous innovation. They become resilient entities, capable of adapting to change and overcoming challenges with grace and integrity.

Commitment to Continuous Improvement and Learning

Embracing lifelong learning and personal development

Lifelong learning is the continuous pursuit of knowledge and skills throughout one's life. For leaders, this journey is crucial, fostering adaptability, innovation, and resilience. The Quran encourages this quest for knowledge, underscoring its eternal importance.

> *"And say, 'My Lord, increase me in knowledge.'" (Quran 20:114)*

This verse encapsulates the spirit of lifelong learning, a principle deeply embedded in Sunnah-inspired leadership.

Personal development involves a deep commitment to self-awareness, goal setting, and the cultivation of skills and qualities that enhance leadership effectiveness. It requires a proactive approach and a willingness to step out of one's comfort zone.

Prophet Muhammad (PBUH) exemplified personal development through his continuous quest for knowledge, self-reflection, and improvement. His leadership was marked by humility, patience, and a constant striving for excellence.

> *"Seek knowledge from the cradle to the grave." (Al-Tabarani)*

This hadith highlights the importance of lifelong learning and personal growth, a core aspect of Sunnah-inspired leadership.

Reflecting on continuous improvement and lifelong learning reveals their profound impact on leadership. Leaders who embrace these principles are better equipped to navigate complexities, drive innovation, and foster a culture of excellence.

Leaders committed to continuous improvement are better prepared to adapt to change and overcome challenges. Their ongoing pursuit of knowledge equips them with the tools and insights needed to navigate uncertainties with confidence.

Continuous learning stimulates creativity and innovation. Leaders who expose themselves to diverse perspectives and new ideas inspire their teams to think outside the box and develop innovative solutions.

Leaders who demonstrate a commitment to personal growth earn the respect and trust of their teams. Their dedication to learning and self-improvement sets a positive example, encouraging employees to pursue their own development.

The principles of continuous improvement and lifelong learning extend to the organisational level. Leaders who champion these values create an environment where continuous learning is embedded in the culture, driving sustained organisational success.

Personal development begins with setting clear, achievable goals. Leaders should identify areas for improvement and establish specific, measurable objectives to guide their growth.

Feedback is essential for personal growth. Leaders should actively seek constructive feedback from peers, mentors, and team members, and reflect on this input to identify strengths and areas for improvement.

Leaders should commit to continuous learning by pursuing formal education, attending workshops and conferences, and engaging in self-directed learning activities such as reading and online courses.

A growth mindset involves believing that abilities can be developed through dedication and hard work. Leaders with a growth mindset view challenges as opportunities to learn and grow.

A support network of mentors, peers, and professional associations can provide guidance, encouragement, and resources for personal development. Leaders should actively seek out and nurture these relationships.

The journey of lifelong learning and continuous improvement transforms leaders into more effective, empathetic, and inspiring individuals. It fosters a culture of excellence and resilience within organisations, driving sustained success and positive impact.

This journey transforms not only the individual leader but also the organisations and communities they serve. It is a testament to the enduring power of knowledge and growth, shaping leaders into beacons of inspiration, resilience, and integrity.

The legacy of Prophet Muhammad (PBUH) provides a timeless guide, reminding us that true leadership is not measured by immediate achievements but by the lasting impact it leaves on the hearts and minds of people. Embracing the principles of lifelong learning and personal development ensures that our influence as leaders endures, creating a ripple effect of positive change that extends far beyond our tenure.

Sustaining Sunnah-based leadership practices for long-term success

As we reach the end of this journey through Sunnah-inspired leadership, it becomes evident that the principles and values derived from the teachings of Prophet Muhammad (PBUH) offer a timeless and profoundly impactful framework for guiding modern organisations and communities. Reflecting on what we have learned throughout this exploration, we find that sustaining these principles is not only crucial for immediate success but also for creating a lasting legacy of ethical leadership and societal well-being.

The teachings of the Prophet (PBUH) are deeply rooted in core values such as honesty, integrity, compassion, justice, and continuous improvement. These values, when integrated into leadership practices, create a powerful and sustainable model that transcends time and geography. By embracing these principles, leaders can build organisations that are not only successful but also resilient, ethical, and deeply connected to their communities.

One of the most significant lessons we have learned is the importance of honesty and integrity in leadership. The Prophet Muhammad (PBUH), known as Al-Amin (the Trustworthy), exemplified these virtues in all aspects of his life. His commitment to truthfulness and transparency earned him the trust and respect of those around him. In modern leadership, maintaining this level of integrity is crucial for building trust within an organisation. Trust fosters open communication, collaboration, and a sense of security among team members. It also enhances an organisation's reputation, attracting customers, investors, and talented employees who value ethical conduct.

Compassion and inclusivity are also central to Sunnah-based leadership. The Prophet (PBUH) showed immense empathy and kindness, treating everyone with respect and dignity regardless of their status. This approach not only united diverse communities but also created a supportive and inclusive environment. In contemporary organisations, leaders who prioritise compassion and inclusivity foster a culture where everyone feels valued and respected. This leads to higher employee morale, increased productivity, and a stronger sense of loyalty and belonging.

Justice and fairness are other critical components of Sunnah-inspired leadership. The Prophet (PBUH) consistently upheld justice, ensuring that all individuals were treated equitably. His leadership was marked by fairness in decision-making and an unwavering commitment to doing what was right. In today's business world, leaders who embrace these principles create fair and just workplaces. This means implementing fair wage policies, providing equal opportunities for advancement, and maintaining impartial grievance procedures. Such practices not only enhance employee satisfaction and retention but also contribute to a harmonious and productive work environment.

Continuous improvement and lifelong learning are deeply embedded in the Sunnah. The Prophet Muhammad (PBUH) encouraged the pursuit of knowledge from the cradle to the grave. This commitment to learning and self-improvement is crucial for modern leaders who must navigate an ever-changing business landscape. By embracing a mindset of continuous improvement, leaders can stay ahead of industry trends, foster innovation, and drive organisational success. This involves setting clear personal development goals, seeking feedback, engaging in continuous learning, and nurturing a growth mindset.

A significant aspect of Sunnah-inspired leadership is the focus on social responsibility and community engagement. The Prophet (PBUH) emphasised the importance of contributing to the welfare of society.

> *He said, "The best among you are those who have the best manners and character." (Sahih Bukhari)*

This principle translates into modern leadership through corporate social responsibility (CSR) initiatives that address social issues such as poverty, education, and healthcare. Leaders who prioritise social responsibility not only improve the well-being of their communities but also enhance their organisation's reputation and strengthen community relations.

The legacy of Prophet Muhammad (PBUH) in leadership is a testament to the enduring power of ethical and compassionate leadership. His principles of honesty, integrity, compassion, justice, and continuous improvement provide a timeless guide for modern leaders. By integrating these values into their leadership practices, leaders can create organisations that are not only successful but also resilient, ethical, and deeply connected to their communities.

Reflecting on the journey through Sunnah-inspired leadership, it is clear that sustaining these principles requires a deep commitment to personal and organisational growth. Leaders must embody these values in their daily actions, setting a positive example for their teams. This involves leading with humility, patience, and resilience, and constantly striving for excellence. It also means creating an organisational culture that values ethical behaviour, inclusivity, and continuous improvement.

One of the most profound lessons from this journey is the importance of leading by example. The Prophet Muhammad (PBUH) led by example, demonstrating the values he espoused in his own behaviour. Modern leaders can learn from this by embodying the principles of Sunnah-inspired leadership in their actions. This means being honest and transparent in all dealings, showing compassion and empathy towards others, upholding justice and fairness, and continuously seeking knowledge and improvement. By doing so, leaders inspire their teams to follow suit, creating a ripple effect of positive change throughout the organisation.

Another key aspect of sustaining Sunnah-based leadership practices is the emphasis on community and social responsibility. The Prophet (PBUH) was deeply committed to the well-being of his community, and modern leaders can carry this legacy forward by engaging in corporate social responsibility initiatives. This involves addressing social and environmental issues, supporting local communities, and creating value beyond financial profits. By prioritising social responsibility, leaders can create a positive impact that extends beyond their organisation, contributing to the overall well-being of society.

Sustaining Sunnah-based leadership practices also involves fostering a culture of continuous improvement and lifelong learning. This requires creating an environment where learning is valued and encouraged, and where employees are given opportunities for growth and development. Leaders can support this by providing access to training and development programs, encouraging feedback and reflection, and fostering a growth mindset within their teams. By promoting a culture of continuous improvement, leaders ensure that their organisations remain adaptable, innovative, and resilient in the face of change.

Leaders who embrace this journey enhance their own capabilities and inspire their teams to pursue excellence. This commitment to personal and organisational growth ensures that the principles of Sunnah-inspired leadership are sustained and adapted to meet the evolving challenges of the future.

This journey transforms not only the individual leader but also the organisations and communities they serve. It is a testament to the enduring power of knowledge and growth, shaping leaders into beacons of inspiration, resilience, and integrity.

The lessons drawn from the life of Prophet Muhammad (PBUH) provide a timeless guide, ensuring that the influence of ethical leadership endures for generations to come. By committing to the principles of Sunnah-inspired leadership, leaders can create a legacy of excellence, integrity, and compassion that transcends time and geography.

Let us embrace the wisdom of lifelong learning, striving to be better each day, and inspiring those around us to do the same. In this relentless pursuit of knowledge and improvement, we honour the timeless teachings of the Sunnah, ensuring that our impact as leaders endures for generations to come.

This is the essence of true leadership – a journey of growth, impact, and enduring influence that leaves a lasting legacy of positive change and success. May the teachings and examples of Prophet Muhammad (PBUH) continue to inspire and guide us in our journey as leaders.

Duas for Guidance and Success

O Allah, the Most Merciful and the Most Compassionate, we come before You with humility and gratitude for the wisdom and guidance You have bestowed upon us. We thank You for the timeless teachings of Your beloved Prophet Muhammad (PBUH), who has shown us the path of righteousness, justice, and compassion.

O Allah, grant us the strength to embody the principles of Sunnah-inspired leadership. Help us to lead with honesty and integrity, always upholding the truth and fulfilling our responsibilities with trustworthiness. Guide us to be compassionate and just, treating all those under our care with fairness and empathy.

O Allah, inspire us with the vision and foresight to make wise decisions that benefit our communities and the world at large. Grant us the ability to adapt to change and embrace innovation, so that we may overcome challenges and seize opportunities with confidence and resilience.

O Allah, help us to empower others and foster inclusivity, recognising the potential in every individual and encouraging their contributions for the common good. Teach us to be humble and patient in our leadership, always striving for personal growth and improvement.

O Allah, make us instruments of Your mercy and benefactors of Your creation. Enable us to contribute to the well-being of society through acts of kindness, charity, and social responsibility. May our efforts bring about positive change and reflect the true spirit of Islamic leadership.

O Allah, protect us from arrogance, injustice, and negligence. Keep our intentions pure and our actions sincere, so that we may lead by example and inspire others to follow the path of righteousness.

O Allah, bless our endeavours with success and prosperity. Grant us the wisdom to navigate the complexities of the modern world while staying true to the principles of the Sunnah. May our leadership leave a legacy of excellence, integrity, and compassion that endures for generations to come.

O Allah, we seek Your guidance and support in all our undertakings. Shower Your blessings upon us and our families, and grant us the ultimate success in this life and the Hereafter.

"O Allah, I ask You for forgiveness and well-being."

Ameen.

May these teachings guide us in our personal and professional lives, helping us to become better leaders, better followers, and better human beings.

Let us carry forward the legacy of Prophet Muhammad (PBUH) with unwavering faith, steadfast determination, and boundless compassion.

Find Out More

Website: www.barakahinbusiness.com

Socials: @barakahinbusiness

If you enjoyed this book, kindly leave a review to help expand our reach so others may benefit also.

www.ingramcontent.com/pod-product-compliance
Lightning Source LLC
Chambersburg PA
CBHW071156070526
44584CB00019B/2813